THE SISTER REPUBLICS

Switzerland and the United States from 1776 to the Present

by

JAMES H. HUTSON

Library of Congress Washington 1991

This book, and the exhibition that it accompanies, have been made possible by generous grants from the Swiss government (Co-ordinating Commission for the Presence of Switzerland Abroad) and the CIBA-GEIGY corporation, with the assistance of the Cultural Affairs Office of the Embassy of Switzerland.

Library of Congress Cataloging-in-Publication Data

Hutson, James H.
The sister republics : Switzerland and the United States from 1776 to the present / James H. Hutson. — 2nd ed.
p. cm.
Includes bibliographical references.
"Based on an exhibit called the Sister Republics, at the Library of Congress, May 1991"—P. 6.
ISBN 0-8444-0762-3 (alk. paper)
1. United States—Relations—Switzerland—Exhibitions. 2. Switzerland—Relations—United States—Exhibitions. 3. United States—Constitutional History—Exhibitions. 4. Switzerland—Constitutional History—Exhibitions. I. Library of Congress. II. Title
E183.8.S9H88 1992
303.48'2730494—dc20 92-28579
CIP

COVER ILLUSTRATION: A Swiss Miss, recommending the referendum. (Detail adapted from illustration on page 60.)

Contents

Foreword

From its earliest years the Library of Congress has collected works by Swiss authors. When the Library acquired Thomas Jefferson's library in 1815, it received copies, annotated by Jefferson himself, of the works of two Swiss authors much admired by the ex-president: the natural law theorists Emmerich de Vattel and Jean Jacques Burlamaqui. A noted American scholar has recently argued that some of Jefferson's most arresting phrases in the Declaration of Independence may, in fact, have been inspired by Burlamaqui.

After the acquisition of Jefferson's books the Library continued to collect Swiss books as well as maps and descriptions of Switzerland. Official contacts between the Library and Switzerland began in 1884, when the Librarian of Congress, Ainsworth Rand Spofford, commissioned George H. Boehmer as a special agent to visit European countries to arrange a publications exchange program. Boehmer reached Bern, the Swiss capital, on 20 October 1884, and was buoyed by his conversations with Swiss officials. They not only shared the eagerness of other European governments to exchange official publications; they also proposed to send the Library of Congress additional books. "As regards historical publications," Boehmer reported, "the Government of Switzerland stands preeminent in her promise to supply as complete a collection as can be obtained—a library in itself—of the historical works of that republic."

Historical works about Switzerland were especially welcome in the United States during the 1880s because many Americans were becoming interested in new instruments of direct political democracy, the initiative and referendum, which had been developed by the Swiss. Numerous American reformers saw these instruments as panaceas to rid the nation's political system of the corrupting influences of robber barons and political bosses. By 1918, twenty-three American state governments had adopted either the initiative or referendum or both, an example of political borrowing that for sheer magnitude eclipsed even Switzerland's modelling her first Federal Constitution of 1848 after the United States Constitution of 1787.

The reciprocal borrowing between the United States and Switzerland before the First World War as well as mutual awareness of a common heritage of resistance to foreign tyranny prompted citizens of the United States and Switzerland to describe their relationship as one of "sister republics." The development of this relationship is described in this book by James H. Hutson, the distinguished historian who is chief of the Library's Manuscript Division. The book is based on an exhibit called "The Sister Republics," opening at the Library of Congress in May 1991 to celebrate the 700th anniversary of Switzerland. The Library of Congress, which has enjoyed a long and fruitful relationship with the Swiss, is pleased to join in celebrating an important milestone in their history.

JAMES H. BILLINGTON
The Librarian of Congress

Preface

Considering the vast number of European immigrants who flocked to the New World, beginning in the fifteenth century, the share contributed by the tiny Swiss Confederation cannot have amounted to much, numerically.

It did carry weight, nonetheless, through those individuals who brought powerful contributions to the structural and institutional foundations of the great American democracy.

From the beginning, Americans, rising up to free themselves from the British Crown, could readily relate to the Swiss example of a handful of men battling to affirm their freedoms.

Beyond the similarities in their initial struggles for freedom, the founding fathers of the American nation, and those in Switzerland who were searching for principles by which to govern their very old democracy in modern times, soon found they shared a common outlook.

In Switzerland, starting already in the seventeenth century, certain enlightened souls had labored in vain to show the cantonal governments—over half of them mired in feudal schemes—the road that could lead to the formation of a modern federal state.

The light eventually did dawn on the Swiss, but not until the nineteenth century! It came from the United States which, after the Declaration of Independence in 1776, had adopted its Constitution in 1787.

Several Swiss writers and jurists had provided inspiration through their writings: Jean-Jacques Rousseau, Jean-Jacques Burlamaqui, and Emer de Vattel.

Seventy years later, casting about for a model, the drafters of the Swiss Constitution came across the American document and deemed it the most appropriate.

A complete way of life: the love of freedom through respect for institutions, a great democratic ideal accompanied by a noble spirit—it was all there in the American texts.

What more could the Helvetians have wished for? Thus the two republics became sisters . . . in a fundamental sense!

JEAN-RENÉ BORY, *Director*
Institut national de recherches historiques sur les relations de la Suisse avec l'Etranger
Château de Penthes, Geneva

Translation courtesy of the Cultural Affairs Office Embassy of Switzerland, Washington

Introduction

"Let us be united, as two Sister-Republicks."
JOHANN RODOLPH VALLTRAVERS TO BENJAMIN FRANKLIN, 14 APRIL 1778[1]

"Unsere grosse Schwesterrepublick jenseits des Oceans."
GOVERNMENT OF AARGAU TO THE AMERICAN MINISTER, 28 APRIL 1865[2]

"Votre puissante et admirable republique, que nous sommes fiers d'appeler notre soeur."
CITIZENS OF FRIBOURG TO THE REPUBLICANS OF AMERICA, 13 MAY 1865[3]

In 1776 the government of Switzerland, known to its citizens as the Eidgenossenschaft (community of the oath), had existed for almost five hundred years. The Eidgenossenschaft was a confederacy of thirteen states called cantons, which were republics of various sizes—some democratic, others aristocratic. Republics were rare in 1776. Aside from obscure backwaters like San Marino and from the Netherlands, which many believed had repudiated republicanism, Switzerland had no company in eighteenth century Europe. Many Swiss, therefore, welcomed the Declaration of Independence of the United States, since it ushered a soulmate into the community of nations. Not only was the infant American government a confederate republic, it contained, mirabile dictu, thirteen states. Thus, it seemed natural to Swiss officials like Johann Rodolph Valltravers, councillor of Bienne, to propose in 1778 an alliance between the two countries which would form a "lasting Foundation of Friendship, and of mutual good offices between the two Sisters, the 13 republican states of N. America, and of Switzerland."[4]

Nothing came of Valltravers' proposal, but his convictions about a community of interests between the United States and Switzerland were shared by significant numbers of Swiss in succeeding generations. Thus, it again seemed natural, as the American Civil War ended in 1865, for thousands of Swiss to salute the triumph of their Sister Republic. How, in fact, could the "oldest existing republic in the civilized world," as a Swiss journalist called his country in 1865,[5] be indifferent to the victory of Union arms. As the exuberant American minister, George Fogg, told the President of the Swiss Confederation on May 6, 1865, "the government and people of the Helvetic Republic have never wavered in their friendship towards a greater sister-republic and in fidelity to their own ancient traditions."[6]

Republicanism was not the only bond between Switzerland and the United States. From 1776 onward political developments in one country often paralleled those in the other and each country, on important occasions, served as a constitutional model for the other. The first American national constitution, the Articles of Confederation, was constructed on the Swiss model of a confederacy over sovereign states. When Americans repudiated confederal government in 1787 as impotent and unworkable and adopted a new federal constitution, the opponents of the new charter, the Antifederalists, argued that a Swiss-style confederal government was still a viable model which offered the best hope for the preservation of American liberty.

The Swiss themselves repudiated confederal government in 1848, using many of the same arguments Americans had marshalled against it in 1787 and adopted a federal constitution modelled after the American constitution of 1787. First, however, the Swiss were obliged to fight a civil war in 1847 against regressive (so the victors believed) political and religious forces. Fourteen years later the American Union fought its own civil war against forces that it considered equally reactionary. After the Civil War many American state and local governments adopted constitutional reforms borrowed from the Swiss—the initiative and referendum—which continue to this hour to give the politics of California and other influential states their distinctive tone.

Institutional borrowing between the United States and Switzerland ceased after the First World War. Not long afterwards Swiss and Americans ceased referring to each others' countries as sister republics. There is no better time, the Library of Congress believes, to revive that venerable phrase and to illustrate the fruitful relationship which it described than on the occasion of the 700th anniversary of Swiss Independence and Freedom, which the Library will celebrate with an exhibit, opening in May 1991. Since 1776 Switzerland and the United States have contributed much to each other, so much that we expect that readers of this publication and viewers of the exhibit will be surprised to find that so little of the story is known in this country.

James H. Hutson

NOTES

1. William B. Willcox, et al., eds., *The Papers of Benjamin Franklin*, 26 (New Haven, 1987), 293.
2. George Müller, *Der amerikanische Sezessionskrieg in der schweizerischen öffentlichen Meinung* (Basel, 1944), 196.
3. *Ibid.*, 210.
4. Claude A. Lopez, et al., eds., *The Papers of Benjamin Franklin*, 27 (New Haven, 1988), 158.
5. Müller, op. cit., 192.
6. *Ibid.*, 25.

Washington and Tell. The Heroes of immortal Freedom

Engraving

Original in Universitätsbibliothek, Karl Marx Universität, Leipzig. Photograph courtesy of the University of North Carolina Press, Chapel Hill, North Carolina.

This anonymous engraving, dated by authorities between 1777 and 1793, shows the linkage in the eighteenth century European mind between the national heroes of Switzerland and the United States. The common love of freedom, ascribed to citizens of both countries, as well as certain similarities in government, made the term Sister Republics seem an appropriate description of the two nations.

Swiss and the American Revolution

The Swiss made a significant contribution to the creation of the American Republic. They furnished intellectual weapons to American statesmen and troops and ordnance to Washington's armies. So little is known, however, about their military contribution to the patriot cause that the Swiss can be considered the invisible men of the American Revolution, as anonymous as black Americans were until the scholarship of the past two decades uncovered their substantial participation in the achievement of American independence.

The Swiss were invisible because their language disguised their national identity; most of them spoke German and their American contemporaries assumed that anyone speaking that tongue must, obviously, be a "German." Another reason the Swiss have been overlooked is because they have been undercounted by scholars, who currently assume that no more than 25,000 sons and daughters of Helvetia emigrated to America during the eighteenth century. This figure was proposed in 1916 by a professor of literature, Albert Faust, who derived it by extrapolating from a list of Zurich emigrants to America from 1734 to 1744.[1] No modern demographer would accept Faust's calculations, for they are based on the obvious fallacy that the Zurich experience in that decade was identical to the experiences in all other cantons, i.e., Faust assumes that, if x people left Zurich at a particular time, 2x simultaneously left a place twice as large. The Zurich list, moreover, includes those who left with official permission and paid emigration fees amounting to as much as 18 percent of their property.[2] How many left surreptitiously, to avoid paying these fees, is unknown to Faust or any other investigator.[3] Another problem with Faust's figures is that the "high tide of Swiss emigration to America" occurred in 1749–1754, not in 1734–44, as he assumed.[4]

Faust's most serious error, however, was his failure to account for the Swiss who came to America via other countries.

Ein schön Lied
von dem
Schweizerischen Erz-Freyheitssohn
Wilhelm Thellen,
dem Urheber der Löbl. Eydgenossenschaft.
Samt einem andern Liede
von dem
Ursprung und Herkommen der Schweizer.

Philadelphia,
Nach einem Schweizerischen Exemplar treulich nachgedruckt, und zu finden bey Henrich Miller, in der Zweyten-strasse. 1768.

Paul Weiss.

"A beautiful song about the chief Swiss Son of Liberty, William Tell"

Woodcut

Courtesy of the Historical Society of Pennsylvania

William Tell's famous feat is shown on the title page of a songbook published in Philadelphia in 1768 by Henry Miller (Johann Henrich Möller), the most influential German-language printer in colonial America. A Swiss who served his apprenticeship in Basel, Miller (1702–1782) intended to commend American resistance to Great Britain to his German-language readers by suggesting that William Tell himself would have been a Son of Liberty, the name of organized American opponents of Great Britain in 1768.

Mobility, as Bernard Bailyn has recently written, was "endemic in southwestern Germany; throughout the Rhine Valley [and] in parts of Switzerland"[5] during the late seventeenth and early eighteenth centuries. Many Swiss moved first to the Palatinate or to other parts of Germany and then on to America where their new countrymen considered them as "Palatines." From 1727 to 1734, for example, the official policy of the customs service in Pennsylvania was to call all German speaking arrivals "Palatines," even though boatloads of these Palatines can be shown to have been Swiss.[6] The point here is not that all "Palatines" or "Germans" who entered America were Swiss; a considerable number were, however, and neither they nor any other Swiss who came to America after a stop along the way were counted by Professor Faust. How many of the 200,000 or more "Germans" who are assumed to have emigrated to the thirteen colonies before independence were actually Swiss?[7] We do not know, but the numbers were surely higher than current scholarly computations.

That large numbers of Swiss were among the German-speaking population in America was taken for granted by the revolutionary period's most influential German-language newspaper publisher, Henry Miller (Johann Heinrich Möller).[8] Scholars consider Miller to be the single most influential person in enlisting America's "Germans" in support of the independence of the United States. This "German" tribune of American liberties, Henry Miller, was a Swiss, whose indirect path to America was similar to that of many of his countrymen. Born in 1702 of Swiss parents who had migrated to Rhoden, Germany, Miller moved back to Switzerland in 1715 and served a five-year apprenticeship in the Basel print shop of Johann Ludwig Brandmüller. He traveled around Europe, lived in London, and settled in Philadelphia in 1762. For the next seventeen years Miller published, under various titles, his German-language newspaper which circulated throughout the continent from Halifax, Nova Scotia, to Ebenezer, Georgia.

Unlike the earliest Swiss emigrants, who were primarily Mennonites or members of other pacifist sects, Miller was a Lutheran, then a Moravian, who had no scruples against participation in partisan politics or against bearing arms. He waded into the dispute with the British as soon as it began. His frequent use of heroic men and events from Swiss history to generate support for the American cause indicates that he assumed that a large number of his readers were Swiss. Thus, in 1768, when Sons of Liberty mobilized throughout the colonies to force the repeal of British taxes, Miller illustrated the rectitude of their efforts by printing a "beautiful song" about the "principal Swiss Son of Liberty (Schweizerische Erz-Freiheitsohn)," William Tell, complete with a picture

1776. Freytags, den 26 July. Henrich Millers 818 Stück.

Pennsylvanischer Staatsbote.

Diese Zeitung kommt alle Wochen zweymal heraus, näml. Dienstags und Freytags, für Sechs Schillinge des Jahrs.

N.B. *All* ADVERTISEMENTS *to be inserted in this Paper, or printed single by* HENRY MILLER, *Publisher hereof, are by him translated gratis.*

Das Hölzene Bein.
Ein Schweitzer Hirten-Gedicht.
Von Gessner.

Williamsburg, den 13 July.

Neuyork, den 22 July.

Philadelphia, den 26 July.

Pennsylvanischer Staatsbote, 26 July 1776

Newspaper

Serial and Government Publications Division

In an effort to stimulate martial spirit among his Swiss and German readers, Henry Miller published in the 26 July 1776 issue of his newspaper, the Pennsylvanischer Staatsbote, *a sentimental war story, Das hölzene Bein (The wooden Leg) by the Swiss writer Salomon Gessner (1730–1788). The hero of the story is a survivor of the battle of Näfels, a remarkable Swiss victory over Austrian forces in canton Glarus in 1388, who hobbles through the Alps on a wooden leg, trying to locate the man who saved his life on the battlefield. The disabled veteran finally finds his rescuer's son, herding goats in the mountains, and richly rewards him.*

showing Tell shooting the apple from his son's head in the presence of Gessler and his henchmen.

In 1775 Miller formed a partnership in patriotic propaganda with a fellow Swiss, the Reverend John Joachim Zubly, who had come to Philadelphia to represent Georgia at the Continental Congress. Born and educated in St. Gallen, Switzerland, Zubly was ordained at the "German Church" in London in 1744 and took a pulpit in Savannah, Georgia, in 1760, after living for a time in the Swiss colony in Purrysburg, South Carolina. In 1774 Zubly published a pamphlet in London, *Great Britain's Right to Tax . . . By a Swiss* which Miller distributed in America. In this work Zubly adumbrated a thesis which he would develop in subsequent writings—that Britain's treatment of America was identical to Austria's repression of Switzerland in the epic years of the thirteenth and fourteenth centuries—and advised his British readers to remember, as they boasted of their ability to subdue their colonies, that "all the power of the house of Austria could not re-conquer a handful of Swiss."[9]

In 1775 Miller published Zubly's *The Law of Liberty. A Sermon on American Affairs . . . with an Appendix, giving a concise Account of the Struggles of Swisserland to recover their Liberty.* Simultaneously, Miller translated the appendix into German and issued it as a pamphlet entitled, *Eine kurzgefasste historische Nachricht von den Kämpfen der Schweizer für die Freiheit.* In describing the *Struggles of Swisserland,* Zubly expanded on the Austrian-British analogy, arguing that George III and Leopold of Austria, some five centuries earlier, were following the same policy: "The design was . . . to excite an insurrection among the inhabitants, and then, under pretence of being rebellious, to make war upon them, and entirely to bring them under the yoke . . . in different times and places, tyranny makes use of the same arts."[10] Zubly described the remarkable Swiss victories of the fourteenth century at Morgarten, Sempach, and Näfels, each achieved by a handful of Helvetians over a host of Austrians, and left his Swiss readers in no doubt that the American cause required them to summon the same measure of indomitable courage on behalf of their new homeland. To emphasize the similarities between the Swiss and American experiences, Zubly reminded his readers that Austrian oppression produced a Swiss confederacy "first only of three men, by degrees of three small countries, which increased gradually to thirteen cantons."[11] Thirteen states were, of course, assembled at that moment in Philadelphia to oppose the latter-day Leopold.

For all of his rhetorical fervor, Zubly could not accept independence, because "Republican Government," as he lectured the Continental Congress, "is little better than Government of Devils. I have been acquainted with it from 6 years old."[12] Fearing, in other words, that independence would produce the social turmoil that he associated with republicanism in his native Switzerland, Zubly cast his lot with the King in 1776. Miller never waivered in his support of the American cause and achieved the distinction of being the first printer in the United States to publish the news (5 July 1776) of the adoption of the Declaration of Independence. Three weeks later, to raise the martial spirit among his Swiss readers, Miller printed Salomon Gessner's sentimental war story, "The Wooden Leg (Das Hölzene Bein)," which described the efforts of an aging survivor of the "battle of Näfels in Canton Glarus in the year 1388" to find the man who saved his life on that heroic field. High in the Alps the old veteran, hobbling on his wooden leg, finally found his rescuer's son, herding goats. He gave the young man riches and his beautiful daughter's hand in marriage and the young lovers, naturally, lived happily ever after. Whether Miller's publication of Gessner's story had an equally happy effect in procuring recruits for the Continental Army is unknown.

We do not know how many Swiss bore arms for the United States during the Revolutionary War. It has recently been estimated that between 200,000 and 250,000 men served in American units during the war.[13] George Bancroft assumed that one eighth of the American Army was "German." If this guess—and it is no better than that—is correct, perhaps 30,000 "Germans" fought for American independence. Of these 30,000 "Germans" as many as 10,000 may have been Swiss. The point here is not that Germans and Swiss "won" the War for Independence, only that their role in that conflict can not be overlooked.

In a few cases it is possible to identify Swiss fighting units like Lindenmuth's company, Third Battalion, Berks County, Pennsylvania militia. In a few more cases we know the names of Swiss artisans and merchants who contributed to the war effort. Jean-Daniel Schweighauser of Basel, for example, served during the early years of the war as American consul at Nantes and supervised the shipment of desperately needed French arms and ammunitions to the Continental Army. Some Swiss made rifles for Washington's soldiers in their shops in America. The Pennsylvania or Kentucky rifle, which evolved from the "Swiss-Jaeger" rifle, was apparently "invented" by the Lancaster County, Pennsylvania, gunsmith, Martin Meylin, whose family emigrated from Hedingen, canton of Zurich.[14] Other Swiss gunsmiths in the Lancaster area were expert fabricators of the Pennsylvania rifle and during the Revolutionary War produced these weapons for the Continental Army as well as for state troops.

The war record of at least one Swiss artisan-entrepreneur, John Jacob Faesch, is extremely well documented.[15] Faesch was born and educated in Basel, but moved to Neuwied, Germany, before emigrating to New Jersey in 1764. Characteristically, to Faesch's new countrymen he was not a Swiss but a "smart little Dutchman." Having learned the iron-making business in Germany, Faesch settled in Morris County, New Jersey, one of the best sources of iron ore in the colonies, and by 1773 he was producing high quality iron products at Mount Hope. An ardent patriot, Faesch made iron chains to obstruct the Hudson River and produced various kinds of ammunition, shells, casings, and cannon for Washington's army. According to the commander of the Continental Artillery, Henry Knox, Faesch's armaments were far superior to Pennsylvania-made ordnance and Washington interested himself in Faesch's operations, visiting him at Mount Hope on several occasions. The iron master felt confident enough in his friendship with the General to write him in 1795, recommending a friend for a federal job.

The Swiss furnished American Revolutionary leaders with intellectual weapons every bit as potent as the products of Faesch's forges. The best known Swiss thinker of the Revolutionary period, Jean Jacques Rousseau, had little impact on American statesmen. They were acquainted with some of his books, but his favorite topics were not relevant to their concerns. Rousseau's "celebration of primitive simplicity," a recent scholar has stressed, was "uncongenial for societies that throughout their histories had been trying desperately to escape from exactly that condition."[16] Two other Swiss savants, Jean Jacques Burlamaqui and Emmerich de Vattel, known today only to academic specialists, had substantial influence on American statesmen. Burlamaqui (1694–1748) was, like Rousseau, born in Geneva, but never deserted his native city. He was a respected member of the Geneva Council of State and a professor of ethics and natural law at the city's university. Vattel (1714–1767), a native of Neuchâtel, was a pupil of Burlamaqui and a thinker of less originality. Burlamaqui's major work, *Principles of Natural Law,* was published in French at Geneva in 1747 and translated into English the next year. Vattel's *The Law of Nations, or the Principles of Natural Law* . . . was published in French in 1758 and then quickly translated into English.

Americans quoted Burlamaqui and Vattel frequently in the pamphlet warfare with British partisans which began in the 1760s. Their popularity stemmed from their explication of natural law, a subject which many Americans had not mastered but which they perceived could be used as an antidote to the "new" British constitutional doctrine of parliamentary sovereignty under which the King in Parliament laid claim to absolute authority in his dominions. The Swiss writers were read with heightened attention

Jean Jacques Burlamaqui (1694–1748)

Painting (copy)

Château de Penthes, Geneva

A public official and professor at Geneva, Burlamaqui produced works on the natural law which were widely admired by the leaders of the American Revolution. Thomas Jefferson was particularly impressed with Burlamaqui. American scholars have argued that Jefferson may have borrowed some of the most familiar phrases in the Declaration of Independence (e.g., "the pursuit of happiness,") from Burlamaqui.

François

PRINCIPES
DU
DROIT NATUREL.

PAR

J. J. BURLAMAQUI

Conseiller d'Etat, & ci-devant Professeur en Droit Naturel & Civil à Geneve.

EX RECTO DECUS

A GENEVE,

Chez Barrillot & Fils.

M. DCCXLVII.

Principes du Droit Naturel (Geneva, 1747)

Book

Rare Book and Special Collections Division.

The most widely read of Burlamaqui's works in America.

as the constitutional conflict reached its crescendo at the First Continental Congress in 1774. An observer of the Congress wrote James Madison, 17 October 1774, that "by what I was told Vattel, Barlemaqui [*sic*], Locke, and Montesquieu seem to be the standards to which they refer when settling the rights of the colonies or when a dispute arises on the justice or propriety of a measure."[17]

Two years later Burlamaqui was still a beacon for American statesmen. Although scholars have long been aware that Jefferson admired the Swiss writer, no one has appraised the Genevan's influence on the Virginian as generously as Morton White, who has recently argued that Burlamaqui was the primary source of some of Jefferson's most arresting language in the Declaration of Independence. According to White, Jefferson regarded Burlamaqui as having uttered "the last word . . . with regard to natural law as it affected individuals."[18] Specifically, it is to Burlamaqui that White attributes Jefferson's distinctive alteration in the drafting of the Declaration of Blackstone's trinity of absolute rights—life, liberty, and property—to life, liberty, and the pursuit of happiness.[19] If White is right, the most memorable phrase in the American political vocabulary has a Swiss accent.

The commitment of American lawyers and politicians to natural law and natural rights began to wane in the nineteenth century and, as it did, the influence of authorities on those subjects like Burlamaqui and Vattel diminished. Joseph Story cited both writers with respect in his *Commentaries on the Constitution* (1833)[20] but after the Civil War few Americans consulted the Swiss writers. Today they are known only to academic specialists. History, nevertheless, has been kinder to them than to the Swiss soldiers of the American Revolution who, since their identities were never known, can not even be said to have been forgotten. With the sword and with the pen, the Swiss, nevertheless, played a role in the events of 1776, a role that was certainly more substantial than heretofore realized.

NOTES

1. Albert B. Faust, "Swiss Emigration to the American Colonies in the Eighteenth Century," *American Historical Review*, 22 (Oct. 1916), 43–44. For the use by modern scholars of Faust's figures, see Leo Schelbert's excellent study, *Swiss Migration to America: The Swiss Mennonites* (New York, 1980), 96.
2. Albert B. Faust, *Guide to the Materials for American History in Swiss and Austrian Archives* (Washington, 1916), 5.

3. In 1772, for example, the official in Basel responsible for emigration did not know how many people had left the canton. Faust, *Lists of Swiss Emigrants in the Eighteenth Century to the American Colonies*, 2 (Washington, 1925), 84.
4. Faust, "Swiss Emigration," *op. cit.*, 43. William T. Parsons identifies 1749–54 as the "peak" years of immigration from the "German-speaking areas of Europe" to Pennsylvania. Parsons, *The Pennsylvania Dutch: A Persistent Minority* (Boston, 1976), 59.
5. Bernard Bailyn, *The Peopling of British North America* (New York, 1985), 32.
6. Oscar Kuhns, *The German and Swiss Settlements of Colonial Pennsylvania: A Study of the so-called Pennsylvania Dutch* (New York, 1901), 56; Schelbert, *Swiss Migration*, op. cit., 184–6.
7. For the number of German immigrants to the thirteen colonies, see Lester Cappon, ed., *Atlas of Early American History: The Revolutionary Era, 1760–1790* (Princeton, 1976), 24, 98.
8. The following information about Miller was derived from Willi Paul Adams, "The Colonial German-language Press and the American Revolution," in Bernard Bailyn and John Hench, eds., *The Press and the American Revolution* (Boston, 1981), 162–228.
9. Zubly, *Great Britain's Right to Tax . . . By a Swiss* (London, 1774), 53.
10. Zubly, *Law of Liberty*, 34–5.
11. *Ibid.*, 41.
12. John Adams, Notes of Debates in the Continental Congress, Oct. 12, 1775, in Paul H. Smith, et al., eds., *Letters of Delegates to Congress, 1774–1789*, 2 (Washington, 1977), 166.
13. Howard H. Peckham, *The Toll of Independence* (Chicago, 1974), 133.
14. Herbert H. Beck, "Martin Meylin: A Progenitor of the Pennsylvania Rifle," *Papers of the Lancaster County Historical Society*, 53 (1949), 33–63.
15. Information on Faesch is derived from the following sources: Bernard Koechlin, "John Jacob Faesch, 1729–1799: Swiss Ironmaster-American Patriot-Entrepreneur. His Story and his Contribution to American Independence," unpublished paper in the author's possession; Ernest Kraus, "John Jacob Faesch," *The North Jersey Highlander*, 15 (1979); Sophie Rolston, "The Ford Faesch House," *Morris County* (Spring, 1987).
16. Jack P. Greene, *The Intellectual Heritage of the Constitutional Era: The Delegates' Library* (Philadelphia, 1986), 43.
17. William Bradford to James Madison, Oct. 17, 1774, in William Hutchinson and William M. E. Rachal, eds., *The Papers of James Madison*, 1 (Chicago, 1962), 126.
18. Morton G. White, *The Philosophy of the American Revolution* (New York, 1978), 161.
19. *Ibid.*, 161–66, 219–20.
20. i.e., 3, 722 n.

Swiss and the American Constitution

Having declared independence from Great Britain in July 1776, the thirteen American states faced the problem of establishing a general government. According to John Adams, no one proposed "consolidating the vast Continent under one national Government." Rather the preference in the Continental Congress was to "follow the Example of the Greeks, the Dutch, and the Swiss, [and] form a Confederacy of States each of which must have a separate Government"[1] The Swiss system commended itself to Congressmen like John Witherspoon, the president of Princeton. In a debate in Congress, 30 July 1776, Witherspoon, representing New Jersey, extolled Switzerland as a model of a "well planned Confederacy" which Americans would do well to imitate. "The Cantons of Switzerland," Witherspoon claimed, had never "broken among themselves, though there are some of them protestants, and some of them papists, by public establishment. Not only so, but these confederates are seldom engaged in a war with other nations. . . . A confederation of itself keeps war at a distance from the bodies of which it is composed."[2] Look to Switzerland, Witherspoon urged his colleagues.

Americans who observed the Alpine Republic found models for a variety of policies. Rebutting British charges that the United States' new ally, France, would betray her—a Catholic monarchy, it was claimed, would not keep the faith with a Protestant republic—Benjamin Franklin on 1 July 1778 invoked "the steady Friendship of France to the Thirteen United States of Switzerland which has now continued inviolate Two hundred years."[3] Concerning national defense, Richard Henry Lee advised Patrick Henry in 1785 that a proper program would require that "our leaders engrave upon their minds the wisdom of the inscription upon the arsenal of Berne in

Switzerland—'that people happy are, who, during peace, are preparing the necessary stores of war.' "[4]

These references display a considerable knowledge of Switzerland and Swiss history. Americans acquired their information by reading old, reliable books like Abraham Stanyan's *An Account of Switzerland, Written in the Year 1714* and by consulting a number of new books that appeared in the 1770s: Vinzenz Bernhard von Tscharner and Gottlieb Emmanuel von Haller's *Dictionaire géographique, historique et politique de la Suisse* (Neuchâtel, 1775), Fortune Barthelemy de Felice's multi-volume *Code de l'Humanité* (Yverdon, 1778), and especially *Sketches of the Natural, Civil, and Political State of Swisserland* (London, 1779) by the English churchman, William Coxe.[5]

Swiss scholars vouch for the accuracy of Coxe's facts,[6] even though the author, anticipating the romantic movement of the next century, presented them in a purple prose that seems excessive even for a promoter of tourism. Unlike his fellow cleric, John Joachim Zubly, who described the climate of his native land as "nine months of winter and three months of cold,"[7] Coxe found the Swiss air bracing and continually gushed about the "awful sublimity of this wonderful landscape" and its "singularly wild and romantic vistas."[8] Coxe tended to overlook the authoritarian governments that existed in some of the cantons at this period and celebrated the Swiss as brave, virtuous free men comparable to the Greeks and Romans during their purest republican periods.

Additional information about the Swiss was supplied to Americans by their minister in London, John Adams. In January 1787 the first volume of Adams's *A Defense of the Constitutions of Government of the United States of America* was published, in which he surveyed the political systems in the Swiss cantons, dividing them into "democratical" and "aristocratical" governments. For information on Switzerland, Adams, like most Americans, relied on Coxe but he also used a volume, *Quarante tables politiques de la Suisse*, by Claude Emanuel Faber, a minister at Bischwiller, which has been described as "one of the most erroneous books ever written about the Swiss."[9] Adams's *Defence* arrived in the United States in April 1787 and thus was available during the Constitutional Convention at Philadelphia that summer and during the ratification campaign that followed.

By 1787 those advocating a stronger United States concluded that the Articles of Confederation had failed, that they were, in fact, a "burlesque on government and a most severe satire on the wisdom and sagacity of the people."[10] Why had the Articles failed? Was there some intrinsic defect in confederal government or did Americans lack the political skills to make it work? The Father

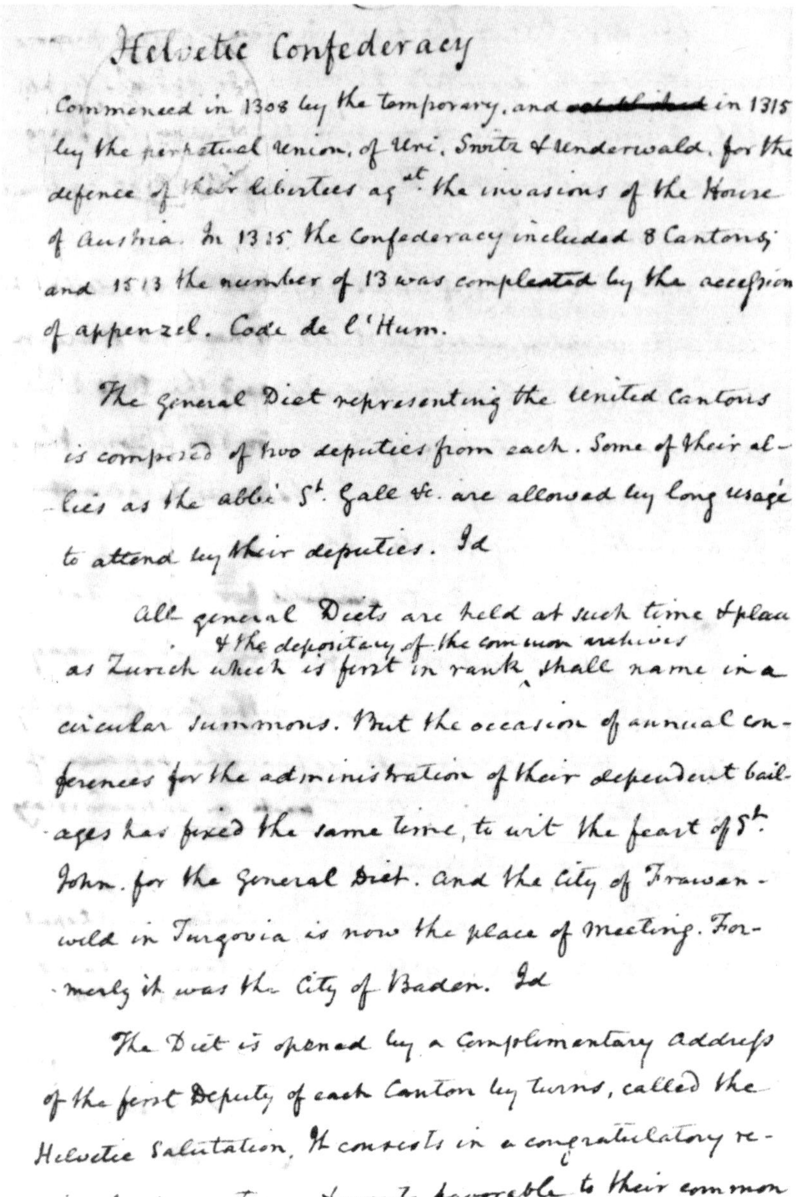

Helvetic Confederacy

Commenced in 1308 by the temporary, and ~~established~~ in 1315 by the perpetual union, of Uri, Switz & Underwald, for the defence of their liberties agst. the invasions of the House of Austria. In 1315 the Confederacy included 8 Cantons; and 1513 the number of 13 was compleated by the accession of Appenzel. Code de l'Hum.

The General Diet representing the United Cantons is composed of two deputies from each. Some of their allies as the Abbé St. Gall &c. are allowed by long usage to attend by their deputies. Id

All general Diets are held at such time & place as Zurich which is first in rank & the depository of the common archives shall name in a circular summons. But the occasion of annual conferences for the administration of their dependent bailages has fixed the same time, to wit the feast of St. John, for the General Diet. And the City of Frawenfeld in Turgovia is now the place of meeting. Formerly it was the City of Baden. Id

The Diet is opened by a Complimentary address of the first Deputy of each Canton by turns, called the Helvetic Salutation. It consists in a congratulatory review of circumstances & events favorable to their common interest - and exhortations to union and patriotism.

Section of James Madison's draft essay, Notes on Ancient and Modern Confederacies

Holograph

Madison Papers, Manuscript Division

In the months preceding the Federal Constitutional Convention which opened in Philadelphia in May 1787 James Madison made a thorough study of confederal governments, ancient and modern, to ascertain if they could be used as a model for the new American constitution (he concluded that they could not). Among the modern confederacies analyzed by Madison was the government of Switzerland—the Helvetic Confederacy, he called it—about which he made several pages of observations.

of the Constitution himself, James Madison, set out to answer this question in 1786. After doing extensive research on the behavior of confederal governments throughout history, Madison drafted his famous "Notes on Ancient and Modern Confederacies" shortly before the Federal Constitutional Convention convened. Madison listed the vices of the confederacies he examined, not sparing the Swiss, whose government, which he called the Helvetic Confederacy, did not "make one Commonwealth . . . but are so many independent Commonwealths in strict alliance. There is not so much as any common instrument by which they are all reciprocally bound together." The absence of adequate central authority, Madison noted, compelled Switzerland to ask an outsider, Victor Amadeus of Savoy, to mediate disputes between the cantons, a "striking proof of the want of authority in the whole over its parts."[11] Here, in fact, was the "vice" Madison found common to all confederacies, a lack of power at the center which had caused the dissolution and subjugation of all ancient confederacies and promised to do the same to modern ones.

The idea of an intrinsic flaw in confederacies, illustrated by Switzerland and other countries similarly governed, was a Federalist theme throughout the debates on the adoption and ratification of the Constitution. Alexander Hamilton, for example, in his great speech to the Constitutional Convention of 18 June 1787, charged that the Swiss had "scarce any Union at all and have been more than once at war with one another."[12] In the *Federalist,* written by both Hamilton and Madison, the "fallacious principle" of confederacies[13] was stressed and Switzerland was cited as an example of that principle in action. *Federalist* 19 asserted that "the connection among the Swiss Cantons scarcely amounts to a confederacy" and claimed that "whatever efficacy the Union may have had in ordinary cases, it appears that the moment a cause of difference sprang up, capable of trying its strength, it failed."[14]

That the Swiss Confederacy had failed was denied by the opponents of the Constitution, the Antifederalists, and as they debated this point with the Federalists, the dispute over the American Constitution at times turned into an argument about the competence of the government of Switzerland. This argument was not, to be sure, a major quarrel, but it is instructive, nevertheless, to record its contours.

Some Antifederalists like Luther Martin applauded the Swiss Confederacy because each canton, regardless of size or population, had an equal vote, a provision that Martin and other Antifederalists obstinately, but unsuccessfully, tried to incorporate into the American Constitution. "Bern and Zurich," Martin asserted at the Federal Convention on 28 June 1787, "are larger than the

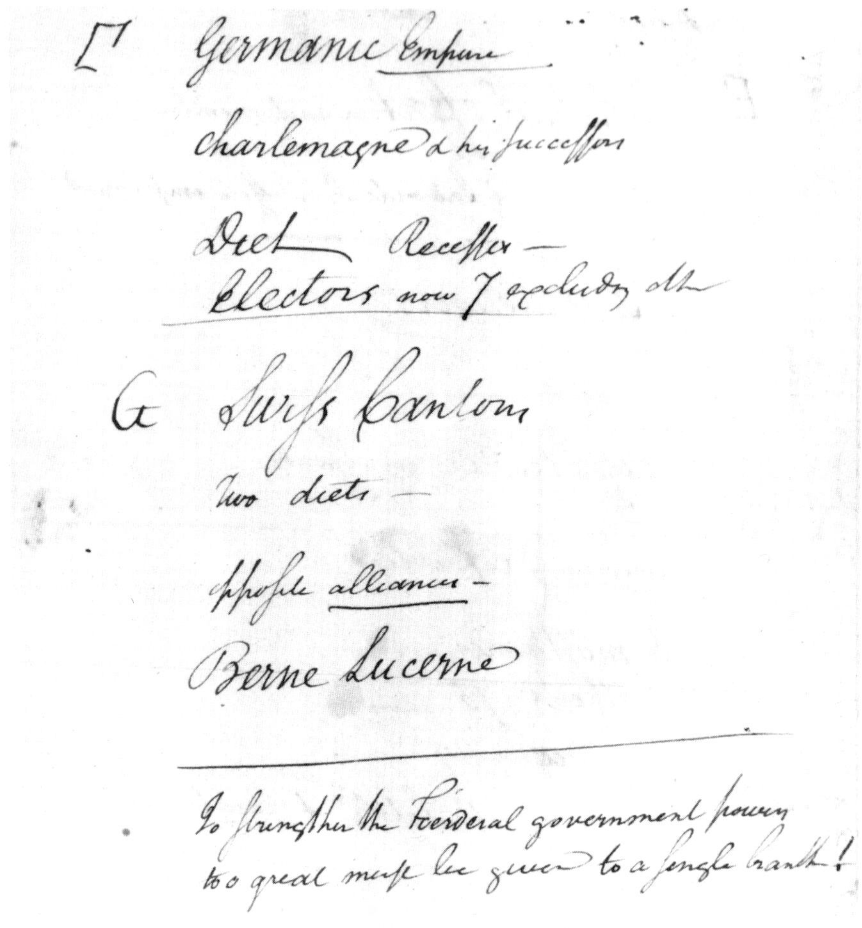
[Germanic Empire
Charlemagne & his successors
Diet — Recesses —
Electors now 7 excluding oth
G Swiss Cantons
Two diets —
Opposite alliances —
Berne Lucerne
To strengthen the Federal government powers
too great must be given to a single branch!

Alexander Hamilton, Notes for Speech in Federal Constitutional Convention, 18 June 1787

Holograph

Alexander Hamilton Papers, Manuscript Division

In his major speech in the Constitutional Convention, 18 June 1787, Hamilton proposed a central government for the United States far stronger than any advocated by his colleagues. He cited Switzerland as an example of what he regarded as an intrinsic flaw in confederal governments: weakness of the central authority, resulting in political instability.

remaining eleven cantons. . . . Bern alone might usurp the whole power of the Helvetic confederacy, but she is contented still with being equal."[15] Other Antifederalists saluted the Swiss because they had managed for centuries without a standing army. But most Antifederalists were drawn to the Swiss because they believed their loose confederacy of more or less sovereign states, contrary to the assertions of the Madisons and Hamiltons of the world, had worked gloriously and proved that Switzerland had been the proper model for the United States in 1776 and continued to be so in 1787.

No Antifederalist boasted more effusively about the success of the Swiss Confederacy than a "Farmer," writing in the *Baltimore Gazette* in March 1788. According to the "Farmer," "these happy Helvetians have in peace and security beheld all the rest of Europe become a common slaughter house;" they "have become in a series of years, passed in uninterrupted but moderate Labor, frugality, peace and happiness, the richest nation under the sun;" they had "remained under the simplest of all forms of government for near five hundred years, in uninterrupted tranquility and happiness."[16] They had, indeed, asserted Patrick Henry in the Virginia Ratifying Convention, for the simple reason that the "Swiss spirit" had remained strong; they had "encountered and overcome immense difficulties with patience and fortitude. In the vicinity of powerful and ambitious monarchs, they have retained their independence, republican simplicity, and valor."[17]

Madison and the Federalists, of course, won the argument with the Antifederalists about the "imbecility" of confederal government, just as Swiss reformers won the same argument with their opponents in 1848. But many historians contend that in the end the Antifederalists were winners, too, for they succeeded in compelling the Federalists to add the Bill of Rights to the Constitution, thereby giving the nation a charter that many consider as valuable as the Constitution itself. In a recent article Paul Widmer has presented the provocative thesis that the Swiss helped inspire the Bill of Rights.[18] Widmer does not mean that Americans looked to Switzerland for model codes of civil liberties. Eighteenth century Switzerland was, he is fully aware, a land in which serfdom and torture in judicial proceedings were still legal and, though far from a totalitarian state, Switzerland, like many of her continental neighbors, was just beginning to be receptive to the full range of Anglo-American notions of rights. What Widmer means is that some measure of the Antifederalists' motivation to demand a Bill of Rights was generated by their admiration for the historic, almost mythic, devotion to liberty that seemed to suffuse Swiss history. Through this channel, Widmer claims, the "Swiss spirit (Schweizer Geist)" flowed into the American Bill of Rights.

Although it may be difficult to document Widmer's specific claim about a link between Switzerland and the Bill of Rights, in a larger sense he is correct in discerning a spiritual communion between Americans and Swiss at the end of the eighteenth century. It is clearly evident in the cultural realm. The first musical, written and performed by Americans, opened in New York City on 18 April 1796. It was William Dunlap's *The Archers, or The Mountaineers of Switzerland*, a dramatic depiction of William Tell and his compatriots, Fürst, Melchtal, and Stauffacher. Several other plays on Swiss themes were also performed before appreciative audiences. The performances were popular because Americans felt a spiritual kinship with the Swiss. No American, declared a theater critic in the *New York Evening Post*, 23 February 1819, could be "insensible" to the story of William Tell. "It is an incident in the glorious struggle of the Swiss for independence. The Swiss were like our fathers, a plain and simple but virtuous, free and valiant nation."[19] To citizens of the young American Republic the Swiss were, to use a term from the modern American vernacular, soul brothers and sisters.

NOTES

1. Lyman H. Butterfield, et al., eds., *Diary and Autobiography of John Adams*, 3 (Cambridge, 1961), 352.
2. Paul H. Smith, et al., eds., *Letters of Delegates to Congress, 1774–1789*, 4 (Washington, 1979), 587.
3. Claude A. Lopez, et al., eds., *The Papers of Benjamin Franklin*, 27 (New Haven, 1988), 5.
4. James H. Hutson, *John Adams and the Diplomacy of the American Revolution* (Lexington, Ky., 1980), 32.
5. For a discussion of the sources of information about Switzerland used by eighteenth century Americans, I have relied upon Paul Widmer, "Der Einfluss der Schweiz auf die Amerikanische Verfassung von 1787," an unpublished paper in my possession. A revised version of this excellent essay has been published in *Schweizerische Zeitschrift für Geschichte*, 38 (1988), 359–389.
6. *Ibid.*, 15.
7. Zubly, *Law of Liberty*, 33.
8. William Coxe, *Travels in Switzerland and in the country of the Grisons . . .* (4th ed., London, 1808–1814), 644, 648.
9. Widmer, *op. cit.*, 15–16.
10. Jack P. Greene, *Peripheries and Center* (Athens, Ga., 1986), 190.
11. Robert A. Rutland, et al., eds., *The Papers of James Madison*, 9 (Chicago, 1975), 8–11.
12. Max Farrand, ed., *The Records of the Federal Convention*, 1 (New Haven, 1987), 285.

13. *Federalist* 18 in Jacob E. Cooke, ed., *The Federalist* (Middletown, 1961), 113.
14. *Federalist* 19, *ibid.*, 123.
15. Farrand, *op. cit.*, 1, 454.
16. Herbert Storing, ed., *The Complete Anti-Federalist*, 5 (Chicago, 1981), 47.
17. *Ibid.*, 227.
18. Widmer, *op. cit.*, 39–41.
19. Heinz K. Meier, *The United States and Switzerland in the Nineteenth Century* (The Hague, 1963), 14n.

Americans and the Swiss Constitution of 1848

If Switzerland furnished models for American revolutionary leaders, the institutional consummation of the American Revolution, the Constitution of 1787, furnished a reciprocal model for Swiss statesmen.

The Swiss followed the course of the American Revolution with attention. Not everyone was as well acquainted with the personalities of the Revolution as the poet Johann Jakob Bodmer who claimed in 1778 that his plays "were completely in Samuel Adams' style of thought,"[1] but most literate Swiss were aware of what was happening across the Atlantic. Their newspapers were "full of America"[2] and books about the Revolution found a ready audience.

Sympathy for the American cause was far from universal in Switzerland. Though more scholarship is needed to establish the point, it appears that the Swiss divided along class lines in their reaction to the American Revolution. The secretary to the British Embassy in Bern reported to his superiors in 1780 that Swiss elites wanted to see the rebellion crushed,[3] apparently because the subversion of authority being achieved by the Americans might prove contagious among restive populations in various Swiss cantons. Their fears were evidently well founded, for scholars have claimed that the American Revolution was the model (Vorbild) for two of the most striking episodes of popular unrest in eighteenth century Swiss history: the peasant revolt led by Nicolas Chenaux against the government of Fribourg in 1781 and the Stäfa affair in the canton of Zurich in 1795–96.

Chenaux's efforts to mobilize the peasants and bourgeoisie of Fribourg to overthrow an entrenched government ended disastrously in May 1781—Chenaux himself was killed and posthumously beheaded, drawn, and quartered. According to an observer, Baron Marie-François d'Alt, the Fribourg rebels were "struck with the great courage of the Americans . . . and made plans strongly resembling theirs."[4] The distinguished historian of Swiss-American relations, William Rappard, contended that the Stäfa Reformers, whose efforts to democratize the government of Zurich were no more successful than Chenaux's ill-fated endeavors, were also inspired by the American Revolution, although other authorities believe they were influenced principally by the French Revolution.[5]

There is no doubt that the turmoil created by the French Revolution focused the attention of many Swiss on the American Constitution of 1787 as a model for their own government. In 1798 French troops invaded Switzerland, rapidly conquered it, and imposed the "One and Indivisible Helvetic Republic." The Helvetic Republic was an example of what the American Antifederalists called a "consolidated" government. The sovereignty and independence of the cantons were abolished and all power was exercised by a five-man directory. The Helvetic Republic did take some "progressive" steps—the abolition of feudal tenures, the establishment of various civil rights—but it was despised by the Swiss as the creation of a conqueror. Few were sorry when it collapsed in 1803.

Many Swiss who opposed the Helvetic Republic did not want to revert to the politics of the old confederation in which cantonal sovereignty had frustrated the achievement of worthy national objectives. What was needed, they believed, was a stronger central government that permitted, as the Helvetic Republic did not, a measure of autonomy in the constituent units. What was needed, in other words, was a federal system such as the framers of the American Constitution had established in 1787. The trauma of the Helvetic Republic made the United States "very fashionable with us," a Swiss commentator noted in 1800.[6] Politicians, academics, and clergymen began extolling the American Constitution as a model for Switzerland. Imitate the Americans, a Lausanne minister advised in February 1800, because they have found it "useful to entrust some legislative and executive power to one national authority [and] no less useful to maintain separate local administrations and to subject to a uniform and central rule only those matters for which that was absolutely necessary in the interests of general prosperity and the defense of the Confederation."[7] The Bürgermeister of Basel, Johann Karl Wieland, was no less enthusiastic about following the Americans. "I know very well that the unitary system does not suit our people," he wrote on 11 September 1802, and "I shall certainly miss no opportunity to endeavor to modify our constitution so as to render it as similar as possible to that of

Ignaz Paul Vital Troxler (1780–1866)

Engraving

Courtesy of the Swiss National Library

A medical doctor and professor of philosophy, Troxler in writings published in the 1830s and 1840s campaigned for the adoption by the Swiss of an American-style federal republic. According to one authority, Troxler "more than any other single person" was "responsible for the adoption of the American bicameral system in Switzerland."

Die Verfassung

der

Vereinigten Staaten Nordamerika's

als Musterbild

der

Schweizerischen Bundesreform.

Mit Vorwort und Erläuterungen

von

Dr. Troxler,

Professor der Philosophie an der Hochschule Bern.

Zum Neujahr 1848.

Schaffhausen.

Verlag der Brodtmann'schen Buchhandlung.

Ignaz Paul Vital Troxler, *Die Verfassung der Vereinigten Staaten Nordamerika's als Musterbild der Schweizerischen Bundesreform* (Schaffhausen, 1848).

Pamphlet

Courtesy of the Swiss National Library

Professor Hans R. Guggisberg has recently noted that in January 1848 Troxler presented this pamphlet, whose title means The Constitution of the United States of North America as a Model for Swiss Federal Reform, to the committee of the Swiss Diet employed in drafting the new federal constitution and that the committee "accepted Troxler's advice on March 22, 1848."

the United States."[8] For the next four decades the discussion of the revision of the structure of Swiss government seldom occurred without the advisability of copying the American constitutional model being considered.

After the collapse of the Helvetic Confederacy in 1803 the Swiss political pendulum swung back in the direction of the old confederation. Under the so-called Mediation of 1803 and the Federal Pact of 1815 the sovereignty of the cantons was restored as was the power of the aristocratic oligarchies that had long governed in many of them. Although it is an exaggeration to say that the Swiss were now "intent on scrambling back into the Middle Ages,"[9] the abolition of many recently granted rights, the imposition of press censorship, and the reintroduction of torture in legal proceedings revealed the cause of liberty to be in retreat.

An abrupt change occurred in 1830. The Revolution in Paris in that year encouraged Swiss liberals to oust the aristocratic leadership in many of the most important cantons and to establish new governments that were based, as was Jacksonian Democracy in the United States, on popular sovereignty. The Swiss liberals were not prepared to open the door of political participation quite as wide as the Jacksonians were—restrictions, for example, were retained on the suffrage and on office holding—but they secured a broad range of rights to their fellow citizens and were committed to the institutionalization of democratic reform.

The liberals and their allies on the left, the radicals, realized that, to secure these reforms in the cantons, the government of the Confederation must be revised and strengthened to counteract conservative efforts from within and without Switzerland to restore the old order.[10] Consequently, in 1832 the liberals persuaded the national Diet to consider changing the national government. The ensuing debates roused advocates of American-style federalism to lobby vigorously for their favorite project. Foremost among the "Americanists" was Ignaz Paul Vital Troxler, a medical doctor turned philosopher, who "more than any other single person [was] responsible for the adoption of the American bicameral system in Switzerland."[11] A prolific writer of pamphlets, Troxler advised his countrymen that after "long and earnest reflections" on Switzerland's problems "a brilliant and happy example of its solution in historical reality loomed up before my eyes. It was the federal system of North America. . . . The constitution of the United States of America is a great work of art which the human mind created according to the eternal laws of its divine nature. . . . It is a model and pattern" for Switzerland and all other republics.[12]

Another pro-American writer, "very widely read all over Switzerland," was the political pastor Thomas Bornhauser of Canton

Thurgau whose pamphlet, *Schweizerbart und Treuherz,* published in 1834, contained the following declaration by the author's protagonist Treuherz: "Even our aldermen here seem to look upon a federal state in which the cantonal and national spheres would be harmonized one with another as a Utopian ideal. Well, the problem has been solved. The United States of North America have founded a federal state in which the freedom of each individual canton stands in perfect harmony with the unity of the nation."[13]

That the American system had captured the imagination of the Swiss public was attested to by James Fenimore Cooper who in his *Excursions in Switzerland* (1836) reported that, although most Swiss were "opposed to consolidation . . . they desire a Union like our own."[14] Further evidence of the popularity of the American system was furnished by a German traveller, Theodor Mundt, who reported that at a political rally of eight thousand Swiss at Langenthal in 1838 he was told by several participants that they had "taken as a model North American constitutional institutions and had especially before their eyes the bicameral system of Congress."[15]

Attractive though the American model appears to have been to many sections of the Swiss public, Swiss politicians were in no hurry to adopt it as the foundation of a new constitutional order. Events conspired in the 1840s, however, to make constitutional revision possible and, in the eyes of many, mandatory. In 1841 the radical government of Aargau suppressed the canton's Catholic convents, which it blamed for obstructing reform. The spark produced by the Aargau incident kindled a civil war six years later. The leading Catholic canton, Luzern, in what appeared to many to be a deliberate provocation, voted on 24 October 1844, to give the Jesuits control over the canton's schools. Assaults by marauding radicals followed and on 11 December 1845, the Catholic cantons of Luzern, Uri, Schwyz, Unterwalden, Zug, Fribourg, and Valais concluded a defensive pact called the Sonderbund, with the avowed purpose of protecting themselves and their religion from outside intervention. To the liberals and radicals the Sonderbund appeared in the same light as the Confederate States of America did in 1861 to Lincoln and his supporters: a secessionist movement designed to support a reactionary institution which must be brought to heel lest the nation perish. As a result, the Diet ordered the Sonderbund dissolved, 20 July 1847, and on 4 November 1847 it sent troops into the field to suppress it. By the end of the month the Sonderbund had been defeated militarily at a surprisingly modest loss in men and material.

In the midst of preparations for war the Diet voted, 16 August 1847, to appoint a committee to revise the constitution. The absence of the Sonderbund delegates in 1847 and their support of

Battle of Gislikon, 23 November 1847

Lithograph by Jules Sulzer de Winterthour

Courtesy of the Swiss National Library

The decisive battle of the Swiss Civil War of 1847 (the Sonderbundkrieg) was fought at Gislikon, 23 November 1847. The victory of the confederate forces led to the adoption of the Constitution of 1848, which was patterned in significant ways after the United States Constitution of 1787.

reform when they reappeared in 1848 guaranteed that the process of drafting the constitution would be controlled by liberal and radical deputies. A constitution was prepared in the winter of 1848, speedily ratified, and put into effect, 12 September 1848. Scholars agree that the constitution, which was voluminous by American standards—114 articles and 7 "transitory provisions"—was, nevertheless, drafted "in conscious and deliberate imitation of the American model,"[16] specifically, in regard to bicameralism and federalism. First, bicameralism: a Council of States, comparable to the American Senate, was established in which each canton had two votes; paired with the Council of States was the National Council, comparable to the American House of Representatives, which was elected by the people at large. To colleagues who were not enthusiastic about bicameralism, the Swiss drafting committee pointed out that "as the task of governing that vast [American] federation is much more complicated and difficult than that of governing the Swiss Confederation, the success made of the experiment of two chambers in that part of the world for more than sixty years past allows us *a fortiori* to hope that it will also prove suitable to our country."[17]

As for federalism, the Swiss Constitution of 1848, like the American Constitution of 1787, converted a league of sovereign states into a federal state in which power was divided between different levels of government: the central government was granted supreme power in some areas, the cantonal governments retained it in others, creating a system that Americans called "dual sovereignty" federalism. The Swiss appeared to imitate the separation of powers written into the American Constitution, although upon closer inspection substantial differences emerge between the operations of the systems in the two countries. The Swiss Constitution of 1848 did, to be sure, establish separate legislative, judicial, and executive departments, but by permitting the legislature to appoint both of its coordinate branches, it deprived them of the independence Americans considered essential for their proper functioning.

The Swiss executive was radically different from its American counterpart. Early in the Constitutional Convention of 1787 the American Framers rejected as impractical a proposal for a three-member executive, representing northern, middle, and southern sections of the country. A single executive, they believed, was indispensable for the success of republican government. The Swiss constitution, however, established a seven-member executive, called the Federal Council, which was, in American eyes, a political heresy of the most egregious sort. The Swiss High Court, the Federal Tribunal, also differed from the American Supreme Court in lacking the power to review laws passed by the national legislative (a power, it is true, not explicitly granted in the American Constitution).

Another difference between the Swiss and American Constitutions was the extent of power given to the central government. Although many of the same powers were granted in both countries—Swiss and American framers, for example, insisted on arming their national governments with control over commerce so that they could promote economic growth—the Swiss were willing to trust their legislature with certain powers—constructing public works, establishing a university—which the American framers specifically withheld in 1787. Finally, the forces which created the American and Swiss Constitutions were strikingly different. Current scholarship in the United States holds that conservative—some would say, aristocratic—elements created the Constitution to thwart democratic movements in the states. In Switzerland, precisely the opposite occurred; democratic forces sought a strong central government to overcome aristocracies in the cantons.

Despite these differences—and it would be possible to mention more—the important fact to remember in assessing the ties between the Sister Republics is that the major institutional features of the Swiss Constitution of 1848—bicameralism and federalism—were copied from the American Constitution of 1787. As a Swiss scholar has recently asserted, one "could almost speak of a plagiary."[18]

NOTES

1. Horst Dippel, *Germany and the American Revolution 1770–1800* (Chapel Hill, 1977), 131.
2. *Ibid.*, 22.
3. *Ibid.*, 221.
4. Georges Andrey, "Recherches sur la Littérature Politique relative aux Troubles de Fribourg durant les Années 1780," in Jean-Daniel Cadaux and Bernard Lescaze, eds., *Cinq Siècles D'Imprimerie Genevoise* (Geneva, 1981), 140.
5. Dippel, op. cit., 338–9.
6. William E. Rappard, "Pennsylvania and Switzerland: The American Origins of the Swiss Constitution," *Studies in Political Science and Sociology* (Philadelphia, 1941), 56.
7. *Ibid.*, 61.
8. *Ibid.*, 64.
9. William Martin, *Switzerland from Roman times to the present* (New York, 1971), 169.
10. Edgar Bonjour, Hilary S. Offler, George Richard Potter, *A Short History of Switzerland* (Westport, 1985), 254.
11. Rappard, "Pennsylvania and Switzerland," 91.
12. *Ibid.*, 93.
13. *Ibid.*, 100.

14. *Ibid.*, 68.
15. *Ibid.*, 107.
16. *Ibid.*, 50.
17. *Ibid.*, 115.
18. Jean-François Aubert, "The United States Constitution and Switzerland," unpublished paper in the author's possession. One similarity between the framers of the Swiss Constitution of 1848 and their American counterparts in 1787 which has escaped the notice of commentators is the "relative youth" of both groups. About the Swiss framers Rappard wrote:

> Ce qui surprend le plus, lorsqu'on évoque le riche passé de la plupart des membres de la commission, c'est leur jeunesse relative. Quatre commissaires, y compris son président, Ochsenbein, et son benjamin, Michel d'Obwald, avaient moins de quarante ans. La grande majorité étaient quadragénaires. Six seulement avaient dépassé la cinquantaine et son doyen d'âge, Abys, n'avait que cinquante-huit ans.
>
> *La Constitution Fédérale de la Suisse* (Neuchâtel, 1948), 111.

In a widely-read article, published in 1961, Stanley Elkins and Eric McKitrick argued that the distinctive feature of the American framers and the source of much of their creativity was their youth. See "The Founding Fathers: young men of the Revolution," *Political Science Quarterly*, 76 (1961), 181–216.

Swiss and the American Civil War

In 1862 the Swiss Consul General at Washington estimated that 6,000 Swiss-born soldiers were fighting in the Union Army.[1] Since as many as 2,300,000 men served in the northern armies during the Civil War, Swiss participation was statistically small. A larger—probably much larger—percentage of Swiss marched with George Washington than with McClellan or Grant. Yet, paradoxically, we know much more about the Swiss who fought in the Civil War than we do about their brethren who served in the Continental Army.

One thing we know is that only a handful of Swiss served in the Confederate Army. A certain Getulius Kellersberger, a colonel in a Confederate engineering corp in Texas, wrote memories about his experiences,[2] but the records are otherwise silent about Swiss in the Southern armies. There is one exception: Major Henry Wirz of Zurich. Wirz emigrated to the United States in 1849 at the age of twenty-six. Eventually settling in Louisiana, Wirz became an enthusiastic supporter of secession, joined the Confederate Army, and was severely wounded at the battle of Seven Pines in 1862. In 1864 he was appointed commander of the prisoner-of-war camp at Andersonville, Georgia, called by one recent Swiss author "the Auschwitz of America" and stigmatized by another as a precursor of the Nazi extermination camps, ("Vernichtungslager des Dritten Reiches").[3] Casualties among the prisoners during Wirz's tenure were so high that after the war the victorious Union government tried him for what would today be called war crimes and hanged him, the only post-war execution of a Confederate soldier or official. Whether Wirz was, in fact, a mass murderer, a "devil in human form,"[4] or a scapegoat for the sins of others, remains to this day a matter of dispute among scholars.

We know more about Swiss in the Union Army. There were several units in which Swiss soldiers were conspicuous. The Fifteenth Missouri Regiment, recruited in St. Louis and nearby Highland, Illinois, contained so many sons of Helvetia that it was called the Swiss Rifles. In battle it carried a distinctive flag which combined the white Swiss cross on a red field with thirty-four stars on a field of blue.[5] Company A of the famous First United States Sharpshooters ("Berdan's Sharpshooters") was mostly Swiss. Its exploits were described in a book, *Drei Jahre in der Potomac-Armee*, published in Richterswil, Switzerland, in 1865 by Captain Rudolph Aschmann, who lost a leg outside Petersburg, Virginia, in July, 1864.[6] Swiss were also sprinkled through the 82nd, 144th and 149th Illinois, the 7th, 9th and 39th New York, the 107th Ohio regiments, and several other units.

Individual Swiss soldiers had memorable Civil War careers. Hermann Lieb, for example, from Ermatingen, canton of Thurgau, rose rapidly from a private in the 8th Illinois Regiment to a major. General Grant put a Mississippi river boat at his disposal so that he could raise a regiment of blacks. In little time Lieb recruited eighteen hundred blacks and organized them into the 5th United States Colored Heavy Artillery which distinguished itself in combat. By war's end, Lieb was promoted to general and commanded the artillery west of the Mississippi. He later became a mainstay in the Democratic Party in Chicago.[7] Even more dramatic was the career of Emil Frey.[8] Scion of an old Basel family, Frey was in Illinois studying agronomy—an imaginative newspaper writer later had him "punching cows"[9]—when the Civil War broke out. Frey enlisted in the 24th Illinois Regiment, commanded by Friedrich Hecker, and later served as a captain in the 82nd Illinois. Captured at Gettysburg, Frey was imprisoned for eighteen months in Libby Prison in Richmond. His confinement was rigorous because he was held as a hostage for a Confederate officer condemned to death by a Union court-martial. For some months Frey and two other men were confined in the "black hole" where they were forced "to catch and eat rats which swarmed in our cell." Frey later recalled that "the negro who cleaned out the cell in the morning was sometimes good enough to roast for us that awful game."[10] Returning to Switzerland after the war, Frey had a successful political career. In 1882 he was appointed first Swiss minister to the United States and in 1894 he became President of the Swiss Confederation.

The Civil War, understandably, made a lasting impression on Frey and his fellow Swiss soldiers. In 1899 a reunion of Swiss war veterans was held at Luzern. Sixteen survivors appeared. They made sentimental speeches and, to rekindle old memories, dined on a menu of "Potage Purrée de Libby beans, vol-au-vent à la Gettisburgh [and] Filet piqué (importé de Chickamauga)." For dessert the old soldiers had "Texas Leckerli."[11]

Some Swiss soldiers joined the Union Army for money and excitement. Others considered they owed the United States a

David Habbegger

Photograph

Courtesy of Mrs. F. L. Habbegger, Highland, Illinois

David Habbegger enlisted in the Union Army at Highland, Illinois, a Swiss community near St. Louis which furnished many members of 15th Missouri Regiment, the Swiss Rifles, whose distinctive flag featured the Swiss cross on a red field and 34 stars on a blue field. Habbegger himself was a saddler in the 16th Illinois Cavalry.

debt of gratitude. "Are not Switzerland and the United States sisters," they reasoned. "Have not thousands of our compatriots found a new, equally beautiful homeland across the wide sea?"[12] Still others claimed that their motives were idealistic. Frey said he was "inspired by the idea of supporting the great cause of the republic."[13] Rudolph Aschmann thought it "glorious to fight for an idea that is destined to bring freedom to all men."[14]

The sensitivity of the Swiss soldiers to the issues at stake in the Civil War was just as keen in Switzerland itself, for a sizeable band on the political spectrum there—the radical and liberal parties—considered that they had a deep ideological stake in the outcome in America. The Union, they believed, was fighting on a more massive scale the same battle they had fought fourteen years earlier against the uncompromising forces of local sovereignty, mobilized on behalf of a morally intolerable institution. The United States, wrote the *Gazette de Lausanne* in a prescient article of 31 May 1861, "is faced with the crisis we confronted in 1847 in the war of the Sonderbund. In Switzerland the quarrel was over the Jesuits; in the United States it is about Negroes. The result will probably be the same: the consolidation and aggrandizement of the central power. . . . It is a repetition *en grand* of our history during the years 1845 to 1848."[15]

The losers in the Sonderbund war, the catholic-conservative cantons, also saw history repeating itself in America. They sympathized with the South in its desire for state sovereignty, but rejected slavery on religious grounds; their attitude toward the Southern Confederacy was, therefore, ambivalent. Only among the textile manufacturing interests in Zurich was there undiluted support for the South and for secession.

Many Swiss supporters of the Union, especially in the radical camp, believed that the cause of the North was, literally, their own cause. If the Union failed, Swiss radicals feared that their own experiment in republican federalism, which was modelled after the United States, would be discredited and would become vulnerable to foreign or domestic foes. The success of the South would "threaten freedom even in their own house," Swiss radicals declared.[16] The Confederacy was denounced as a "death threatening cancer in the body of common freedom," a menace to the "life nerve (Lebensnerv) of the Republic itself."[17] The cause for which the Union fought, Swiss radicals claimed, was "nothing more or less than our own life principle."[18] The radicals became anxious when the Union appeared to falter, as it did early in 1863; they trembled, wrote the *Basler Nachrichten*, about the "future of the greatest, most powerful, most beautiful Free state of the world and of all time." They prayed that a "spirit might arise like Washington's,

Prisoner of war

Photograph

Courtesy of the Staatsarchiv, Basel

This photograph was found in the papers of Emil Frey, the first Swiss minister to the United States (1882) and President of the Swiss Confederation (1894). A captain in the 82nd Illinois Regiment, Frey was captured at Gettysburg and held for eighteen months in Libby Prison, Richmond, one of the many notorious Confederate jails. Frey spent some of his confinement in the "black hole," subsisting on cooked rats, and looked like the forlorn figure in this photograph during the harsh conditions of his captivity.

simultaneously strong and gentle," a spirit that would save the Union in its hour of peril.[19]

The radicals were jubilant when the Union prevailed in 1865. They channeled their exuberance into the "Adressenbewegung" (Address movement) in which twenty thousand Swiss from all walks of life—from men's choirs, rifle clubs, workers' clubs—signed more than three hundred petitions, sympathizing with the sister republic on the loss of Lincoln and congratulating it for its momentous victory over secession which forever "validated the intrinsic strength of republican institutions."[20] These petitions were delivered to the American minister in Bern and transmitted by him to the President and Congress. Their flavor can be appreciated by sampling the most influential address, the widely copied Bern manifesto, written by Florian Gengel, editor of the *Bund*.

> On your side of the Ocean now stands reborn a powerful, great republic, superior to all enemies. With indigenous strength has the American people conquered the disease that toppled the splendid republics of antiquity and threatened it with ruin. Rejuvenated, the American republic stands for eternity, the model and shield of freedom. The republic will be free in the future and in history. Who can still deny that republics can exist among large numbers of people. This victory is a world historical event, an event for all mankind . . . the hearts of all free men beat faster in the elevated hope that the cause of freedom will also be victorious in Europe; above all the Swiss rejoice that the victory is a guarantee that the republic will never fail but will put down deeper roots . . . let our principle be that both sister republics may be united. The cause of democracy and of the republic must prevail!"[21]

George Müller has aptly described the address movement as "unofficial politics, direct spiritual contact between one people and another."[22] But Swiss radicals wanted something more substantial than spiritual communion to commemorate the victory of the sister republic. They wanted something that would place their country's "new Connection with the United States in the spirit of freedom and republicanism eternally before the Eyes" of their fellow citizens.[23] They hit upon the idea of commissioning a well-known Solothurn painter and radical sympathizer, Frank Buchser, to paint a large mural at the Federal Palace at Bern of the leading figures of the American Civil War; juxtaposed with the Americans would be an equally large mural of the heroes of Swiss history. Thus the "living Sympathy and Friendship between both republican nations" would be commemorated by a "visible and lasting monument."[24]

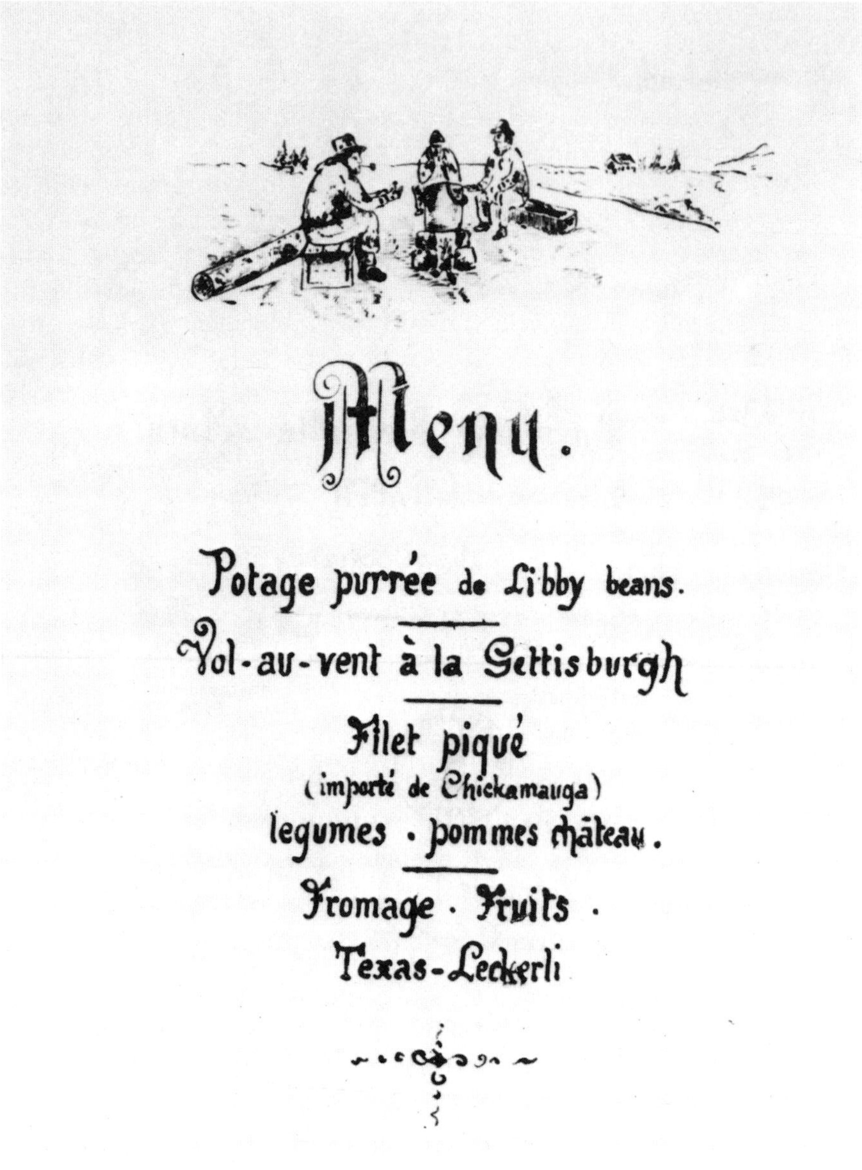

Menu.

Potage purrée de Libby beans.

Vol-au-vent à la Gettisburgh

Filet piqué
(importé de Chickamauga)
legumes · pommes château.

Fromage · Fruits ·
Texas-Leckerli

Menu, Swiss Union Army veterans' reunion, 1899

Printed document

Courtesy of the Staatsarchiv, Basel

On 22 January 1899, a group of Swiss veterans of the Union Army assembled for a reunion luncheon at Muth's Bavarian Beerhall in Luzern. The menu reminded the old soldiers of past battles and experiences. Leckerli is a Swiss cake, a kind of sweet biscuit, often with icing.

The radicals organized a fundraising campaign and sent Buchser to the United States with letters of introduction to various luminaries. He painted President Andrew Johnson, Secretary of State William Seward, and Generals Grant, Lee, and Sherman. Buchser was impressed with the military men, all of whom were of "more value than these intriguing sneakers and profane swindlers [and] wirepullers who hereabouts are called politicians."[25] Although the project of the Civil War mural in the Federal Palace never materialized, Buchser's paintings of Generals Lee and Sherman now hang on the walls of the Swiss ambassador's residence in Washington, a memorial to an earlier age's sense of community between the sister republics.

NOTES

1. George Müller, *Der amerikanische Sezessionskrieg in der schweizerischen öffentlichen Meinung* (Basel, 1944), 22.
2. Getulius Kellersberger, *Erlebnisse eines schweizerischen Ingenieurs in Californien, Mexico und Texas zur Zeit des amerikanischen Bürgerkrieges, 1861–1865* (Zurich, 1896).
3. Karl Lüönd, *Schweizer in Amerika: Karrieren und Misserfolge in der Neuen Welt* (Olten, 1979), 136, 131.
4. *Ibid.*, 133.
5. Robert Gerling, *Highland: An Illinois Swiss Community in the American Civil War* (Highland, Ill., 1978), 7.
6. See also Wiley Sword, *Sharpshooter* (Lincoln, R.I., 1988).
7. For Lieb, see Albert Bartholdi, compiler, *Prominent Americans of Swiss Origin* (New York, 1932), 82–4.
8. For an excellent account of Frey, see Hans R. Guggisberg, "The Unusual American Career of the Swiss Politician Emil Frey (1838–1922)," Swiss American Historical Society *Newsletter*, 22 (June 1986), 3–43.
9. *Washington Herald*, Jan. 12, 1908.
10. *Ibid.*
11. The menu is in the Frey Archives, 485 D, VIII, 4, Staatsarchiv, Basel.
12. Heinz K. Meier, *Memoirs of a Swiss Officer in the American Civil War* (Bern, 1972), 31–2.
13. Heinz K. Meier, *The United States and Switzerland in the Nineteenth Century* (The Hague, 1963), 86.
14. Meier, *Memoirs of a Swiss Officer*, op. cit., 25.
15. Müller, op. cit., 25.
16. *Ibid.*, 43.
17. *Ibid.*, 43–5.
18. *Ibid.*, 36.
19. *Ibid.*, 58.
20. *Ibid.*, 82.
21. *Ibid.*, 191–3.

22. *Ibid.*, 171.
23. *Ibid.*, 82.
24. *Ibid.*, 82.
25. Meier, *United States and Switzerland, op. cit.*, 89.

Swiss-American Peacemaking: the Alabama Affair and the League of Nations

The impact of the American Civil War continued to be felt in Switzerland long after the last signature was subscribed to the congratulatory addresses of 1865; fifty years later, in fact, a famous wartime incident helped persuade an American President to establish the League of Nations on Swiss soil.

A world organization to promote peace was the last thing on the minds of Confederate agents when they commissioned a Liverpool shipyard to build an armed vessel in 1862, ostensibly for service in the Chinese navy. Ship 290, as she was called, slipped out of Liverpool on July 28, 1862, and, christened the *Alabama* on the high seas, set a course that ended in the Geneva Town Hall ten years later.[1] Commanded by Raphael Semmes, the *Alabama* scoured the seas for Union shipping. She captured more than sixty merchantmen, burning many on the spot. The Union government considered Semmes and his crew to be pirates and the British, who had apparently connived at their mission, to be little better. The American minister in London, Charles Francis Adams, threatened the British with war, if they allowed the Confederates to take possession of additional commerce destroyers and, from 1863 onwards, Adams pressed the British Foreign Minister, Lord Russell, to submit the depredations of the *Alabama* and other confederate corsairs to international arbitration. Desiring to appease the American government which had emerged from the Civil War with a powerful army and, the British feared, an appetite for Canada,

The Apple of Discord at the Geneva Tribunal

Cartoon by Thomas Nast, *Harper's Weekly*, 5 October 1872.

Prints and Photograph Division.

The famous American cartoonist, Thomas Nast, uses a William Tell theme to depict the Alabama Arbitration in Geneva in 1872. Imitating Tell, John Bull (Great Britain) shoots an apple, labelled Alabama claims, off the head of Uncle Sam; the feathers of the British arrow, lower right, are marked 15,500,000 in gold, the indemnity levied against Britain by the arbitration panel, whose five members sit watching the proceedings, with Geneva and Lake Leman in the background.

Queen Victoria's government in May 1871 signed the Treaty of Washington which bound the United States and Britain to submit American claims for damages inflicted by the *Alabama* to a tribunal, composed of arbitrators from five nations, which would meet in Geneva in 1872.

The Americans selected Charles Francis Adams to represent them. The British appointed Lord Chief Justice Alexander Cockburn. Brazil picked its ambassador to France, Baron d'Itajuba. Italy named a distinguished jurist, Count Sclopis. The fifth member, representing Switzerland, was none other than Jacob Staempfli, who in 1865 had been a leading spirit in promoting Frank Buchser's trip to America to paint the portraits for the mural in the Swiss Federal Palace at Bern.[2] Staempfli's passionate support for the North during the Civil War was well known to the British delegates at Geneva whose leader, Cockburn, denounced him as a "fanatical republican who detests monarchical governments and ministers to a high degree; he is as ignorant as an ass and as stubborn as a mule."[3] The British correctly feared that Staempfli's pro-Union sympathies would dispose him to support the American position during the Geneva negotiations.

After protracted wrangling during the summer of 1872, the Geneva tribunal awarded the United States $15,500,000 for damages inflicted by the *Alabama* and other Confederate raiders over which the British were judged to have exercised insufficient control. Hotheads in both the United States and Britain denounced the settlement as a betrayal of national honor, but the great body of public opinion in both countries approved it and Britain promptly paid the indemnity assessed it by the tribunal.

Geneva charmed the crowds of journalists who covered the proceedings. "Switzerland," reported the correspondent from *Harper's Weekly*, 26 October 1872, "has indeed been a most hospitable host, and the members of the Court of Arbitration had no cause to complain of dullness during their three months' sojourn at Geneva. Party succeeded party, fete followed fete; and while we used to read in one telegram that the court, quite exhausted by its hard labors, had adjourned to such a date, we learned in another of a pleasant picnic in the environs, or the programme for a forthcoming fishing excursion. In short, both government and people spared no pains to make the stay of their distinguished guests as pleasant and comfortable as possible."

The events at Geneva also made a strong impression on statesmen and jurists who were seeking to persuade governments to resolve their differences peacefully. The successful arbitration of an inflammatory issue by a great power and one fast reaching that status raised hopes that a device had been found to cure nations of

Geneva, astride the River Rhone . . . , June 1919

Photograph, *The National Geographic Magazine*, June 1919.

General Collections

This unusual view of Geneva, looking eastward from the Rhone River, reveals a "flotilla of laundry boats . . . with linen hung out to dry on the docks." Illustrating an article about Geneva as the home of the League of Nations, the picture appears to reveal a premonition of the article's author that "dirty linen"—hence problems—might plague the new organization.

their warring madness. Geneva and by extension Switzerland were henceforth considered oases of hope by men of good will. A report published late in 1872 promoted Geneva as an ideal site for a conference on international law, since it was "recommended not only by its admirable situation . . . but even more by the recent souvenir of the . . . Anglo-American arbitration."[4] The irenic reputation of Switzerland had become so familiar by 1894 that an American writer mentioned the country as "ever a fitting centre for international peace congresses, arbitration courts, and postal unions."[5]

When Woodrow Wilson arrived in Europe at the end of the First World War, citizens of Switzerland as well as every other European country inundated him with good wishes and supplications. Swiss children sent the American President Christmas cards. Switzerland's Armenian community (in common with Greeks, Macedonians, Poles, and other Swiss ethnic groups) implored Wilson to liberate their homeland as part of his crusade to "free humanity and to achieve the work of world regeneration."[5] Revealing the divided affections of Switzerland during the war, French-Swiss organizations, dedicated to "good and durable relations with France and the allied nations,"[7] made Wilson an honorary member of their clubs even as German-Swiss groups sent him petitions, imploring him to lift the "Hunger-Blockade" of Germany.[8]

The Swiss government had its own agenda in dealing with Wilson: preservation of Swiss neutrality and establishment of the prospective League of Nations at Geneva. Working through Professor William Rappard of the University of Geneva and through other emissaries, Swiss officials were successful on both counts. As presiding officer of the Crillon Commission, which devised the structure of the League, Wilson commanded decisive influence on the question of where the organization's headquarters would be. He seems to have favored Geneva from the beginning. As a prolific writer on American history, Wilson was, of course, familiar with the Alabama negotiations of 1872. He had also, apparently, received communications from Geneva in which "the memory of the Alabama arbitration was invoked by the city fathers."[9] Nevertheless, in publicly justifying his preference for Geneva rather than Brussels, Wilson mentioned only the Red Cross, founded by Swiss citizens in Geneva in 1864 and joined by the United States in 1882, as proving the Swiss aptitude for organizing and accommodating multinational ventures in peacemaking and philanthropy. Addressing the Crillon Commission at the crucial moment, 10 April 1919, in its discussions about the site of the League, Wilson declared:

> We wish to rid the world of the sufferings of war. We should not obtain this result if we chose a town [Brussels] where the memory of this war would prevent impartial

> discussion. The peace of the world could not be secured by perpetuating international hatreds. Geneva was already the seat of the International Red Cross, which had placed itself at the service of both groups of belligerents, and which, so far as possible, had remained unaffected by the antipathies provoked by the war. Moreover, Switzerland was a people vowed to absolute neutrality by its constitution and its blend of races and languages. It was marked out to be the meeting-place of other peoples desiring to undertake a work of peace and cooperation. The choice of Geneva did not mean that we did not recognize the eminent merits of Belgium and of Brussels. . . . The capitals of other neutral nations might have been proposed, but none had behaved so impartially as Switzerland. Switzerland had always acted with dignity; she had suffered from the war and she had gained the respect of both groups of belligerents.[10]

Wilson's argument prevailed and Geneva was selected to host the League of Nations. Thanking the American President for using his "powerful influence" on Geneva's behalf, Gustave Ador, President of the Swiss Confederation, assured Wilson that the "Swiss nation, which has already received so many tokens of sympathy from you, will remember that the designation of Geneva is a new proof of a kindness and friendship which are infinitely precious to it."[11]

Apparently believing that Americans needed to know more about the League's home, the *National Geographic* ran an article in June 1919 in which it announced that Geneva would "be known henceforth as the Millennial city. If the League succeeds, the Swiss municipality will become the city set on a hill, the center of man's moral universe." "Geneva," the *Geographic* continued, "now becomes the fountain-head of what may be either the most noble triumph or the most colossal failure in the history of human endeavor."[12] The magazine evidently suspected that the latter result was possible, for its picture of the city was full of premonition. The picture showed Geneva, looking eastward from the Rhone River; anchored in the river in the foreground of the picture was a "flotilla of laundry boats . . . with linen hung out to dry on the decks."[13]

Did the *Geographic* foresee that the League of Nations would be the site of dirty linen—a victim of the refusal of the United States to join and, later, of its own failure to muster the will to confront fascism? These tragedies were not the fault of the Swiss or of Geneva, but the hollowness of the hopes that the millennium would arrive on the shores of Lake Leman were exposed within a few years of the League's founding. By the late 1930s the organization was as dead as the *Alabama*, resting on the floor of the Atlantic off Cherbourg, France, where it had been sunk by the U.S.S. *Kearsage* in 1864.

NOTES

1. The information on the Alabama affair in this chapter is taken from Ladislas Mysyrowicz, *The Alabama Arbitration, Geneva, 1872* (Geneva, 1988).
2. Müller, *Der amerikanische Sezessionskrieg, op. cit.*, 83.
3. Mysyrowicz, *op. cit.*, 38.
4. *Ibid.*, 49.
5. James W. Sullivan, "Direct Legislation in Switzerland," *Direct Legislation Record*, 1 (New York, 1894), 66.
6. La Colonie Arménienne to Wilson, 12 December 1918, Wilson Papers, Manuscript Division, Library of Congress.
7. Cercle Franco-Suisse to Wilson, 15 January 1919, Wilson Papers, Manuscript Division, Library of Congress.
8. Katholisches Friedeninstitut für Völkerversöhnung, Aufruf . . . für Aufhebung des Aushungerungs-Blockus, 1919. *Ibid.*
9. Mysyowicz, *op. cit.*, 48.
10. Arthur S. Link, et al., eds., *The Papers of Woodrow Wilson*, 57 (Princeton, 1987), 225.
11. Ador to Wilson, 13 April 1919, Wilson Papers, Manuscript Division, Library of Congress.
12. Ralph A. Graves, "The Millenial City: The Romance of Geneva, Capital of the League of Nations," *The National Geographic Magazine*, 35 (June, 1919), 457.
13. *Ibid.*, 458.

Swiss and American State Constitutions

As Frank Buchser travelled with his palettes around the United States after the Civil War, he was repelled by the "profane swindlers" who populated American public life. Buchser's contempt for the politicians of the Gilded Age was shared by millions of Americans who believed that their elected representatives had sold them out to big business and political bosses who together were corrupting the nation's soul. How, the question was incessantly asked in the 1880s by reformers and average citizens alike, could the country be rescued from the clutches of the "interests"? How could republican government itself be rehabilitated? Reformers thought they found the answer in Switzerland, in the Swiss inventions of the initiative and referendum. By 1912, eighteen state governments had adopted one or the other—or both—of these devices of direct democracy, which their proponents frankly admitted had been copied from Switzerland. "It is fair to say," wrote one reformer in 1912, "that there would be no modern revival of the initiative and referendum had it not been for the Swiss example."[1] The president of the People's Rule League of America agreed: "the influence of the Swiss example on the development of democracy in the United States in this era is beyond words to express."[2]

How the "Swiss example" came to America's attention is something of a mystery. According to W. D. McCrackan, one of the nation's foremost champions of the initiative and referendum, the "very name" of these devices was unknown in the United States as late as 1888.[3] The Library of Congress, it is true, in what may have been an inspired anticipation of research trends, sent an official to Switzerland in 1884 with instructions to collect "everything relating to the history of the sister republic" and Johns Hopkins University undertook a similar initiative three years later,[4] but there is no indication that the information acquired by these institutions raised the public's consciousness about Switzerland. The political scientist, E. P. Oberholtzer, hypothesized that America's sudden interest in the initiative and referendum was produced by the publication in 1889 of a semi-scholarly work, *The Swiss Confederation*, by the British minister to Bern, Francis O. Adams,[5] but there is no evidence to support this presumption. Nor is there any evidence that the public paid much attention to dry, scholarly tomes like *The Federal Government of Switzerland: An Essay on the Constitution* (Oakland, California, 1889) by Professor Bernard Moses of the University of California or to John Martin Vincent's *State and Federal Government in Switzerland* (Baltimore, 1891). Whatever set the spark, interest in Switzerland raced like a prairie fire through the United States in the 1890s. One scholar counted at least seventy American publications about the Swiss and their institutions between 1891 and 1898.[6] The Swiss initiative and referendum were, in fact, "hot" journalistic topics in the 1890s which no editor dared ignore. Consequently, every literate American received some exposure to these devices.

Certain Americans, who were not satisfied with learning about Switzerland secondhand, went directly to the source to study direct democracy. James W. Sullivan, for example, whose *Direct Legislation by the Citizen* (New York, 1892) was the most popular tract written on the subject—at least eighteen thousand copies were in circulation by 1896[7]—spent several months in Switzerland in 1889 studying the "unprecedented progress" there, with the object of learning what "in the Swiss governmental experience may be found of value at home."[8] Sullivan boasted that the first draft of his best-selling tract had been read and corrected by "Swiss radicals of various schools."[9] Switzerland became a Mecca for American reformers and political scientists, who "sought inspiration in studying the institutions of the little sister republic."[10] Professor Albert Bushnell Hart of Harvard, for example, travelled to Switzerland in 1894 and reported on direct democracy to the *New York Evening Post*. Another professor, Jesse Macy, visited Switzerland in 1896 and reported his findings to the *American Journal of Sociology*. A certain "Professor" Frank Parsons informed an American journal, after an "extensive" trip to Switzerland in 1906, that "he did not find one man" there who favored repudiation of direct democracy in favor of the "old lobby-ridden system of unguarded representation."[11] General Hermann Lieb of Civil War fame visited his Swiss homeland in the 1890s and returned to Illinois a fervent apostle of the initiative and referendum, urging their adoption at mass meetings organized by the Schweizer Club of Chicago.[12]

This deluge of information about Switzerland gave Americans a crash course in Swiss history and a grounding in the intricacies of the initiative and referendum. They learned that in Switzerland there were different kinds of referenda—obligatory and optional—and that as of 1892 all cantons except Fribourg had one

A Swiss Miss, recommending the referendum

Drawing by Dan Beard, *Cosmopolitan Magazine*, July 1893

General Collections

This illustration appeared on the title page of W. D. McCrackan's "The Swiss Referendum, The Ideal Republican Government," one of a flood of articles published in American periodicals in the 1890s, touting the Swiss initiative and referendum as panaceas for American political problems. The Swiss Miss is offering the referendum to Miss America and her eagle as well as to the governments of Britain (represented by the lion), France, and Germany.

or the other. They were further informed that as of that date fourteen of the twenty-two cantons employed the initiative. The Federal Government, it was explained, had used the optional referendum since 1874, but had just acquired the initiative in 1891.

More important were the results that American enthusiasts claimed the Swiss had obtained by using these devices. Sullivan asserted that their introduction in the 1830s had changed the course of Swiss history. Puncturing the idyllic image of Swiss life prevalent in the United States, Sullivan asserted that until the middle of the nineteenth century the Swiss were "ruthless ravagers and despotic masters of serfs"[13] who were compelled "to revolt against their plutocracy and corrupt politicians who were exploiting the country through the representative system."[14] The results of the revolt, which for Sullivan consisted of adopting the initiative and referendum, were dramatic: "the possibilities for political and social parasitism disappear. The 'machine' becomes without effective use, the trade of the politician is rendered undesirable, and the privileges of the monopolist are withdrawn."[15] The lesson for the United States was obvious: "what the Swiss have done, Americans—even the workingmen—can do, once they learn how."[16]

Writer after writer made the same point: once Americans learned to use the Swiss tools of direct democracy they could save their country's political soul. One angry writer, Henry Allen, whose pamphlet *In Hell and the Way Out* was published in Chicago in 1896, charged that the United States had been cast into a living hell by the "organized selfishness" of the banks, railroads, and trusts and by the politicians they had bought. "It is safe to say," exclaimed Allen, "that no other people have been so egregiously plundered by their so-called representatives."[17] The reign of the Money Power, Allen was confident, could be ended by Swiss-style direct democracy. "For several years," Allen observed, "the eyes of nearly all students of political science, the world over, have been turned toward Switzerland, the ideal republic of the old world. The liberty-loving Swiss have been making an actual test of perhaps the most important problem in the experiment of free government namely: the most efficient method for the expression of the popular will."[18] The Swiss test had yielded the happiest results:

> They have made it easy at any time to alter their cantonal and Federal constitutions. They have cleared from the way of majority rule every obstacle—privilege of ruler, fetter of ancient law, power of legislator. They have simplified the structure of government, held their officials as servants, rendered bureaucracy impossible, converted their representatives to simple committeemen, and have shown the parliamentary system not essential to law-making. They

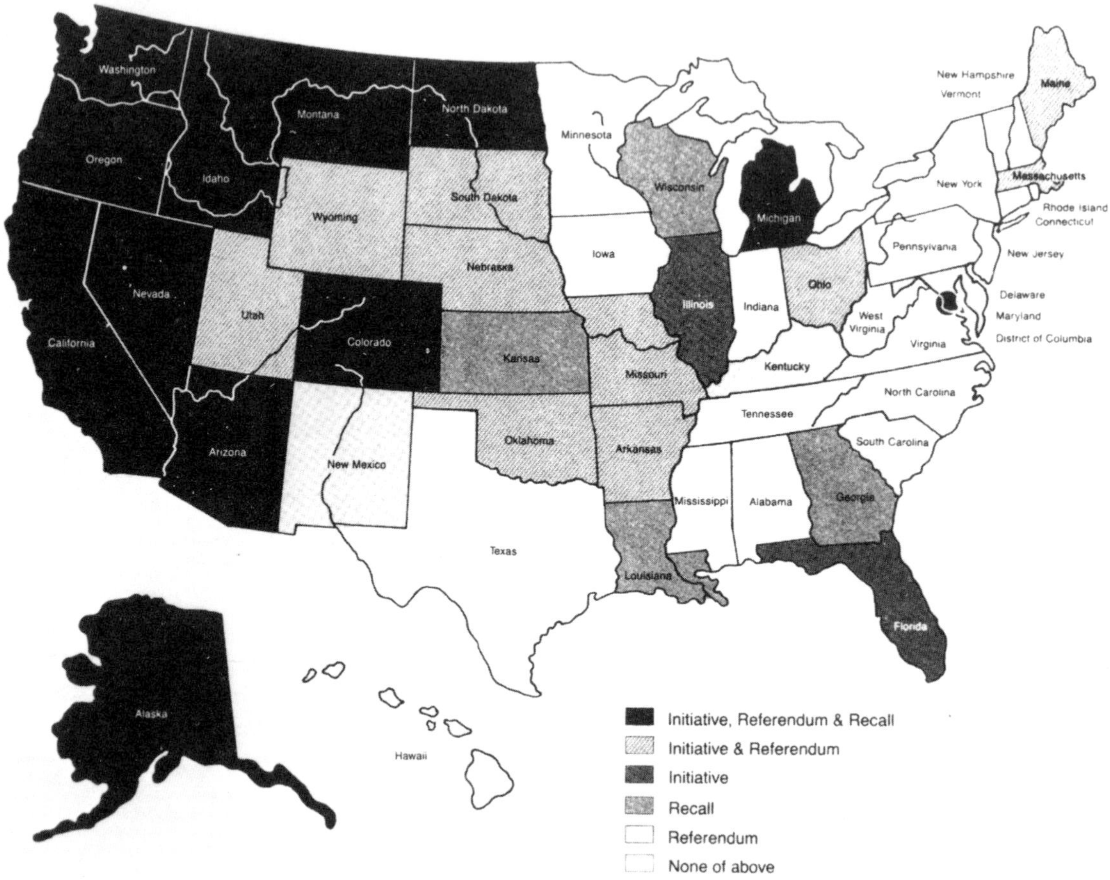

Citizen-initiated initiative, referendum, and recall at the state level.

The Initiative and Referendum in American State Governments

Map, reproduced from Thomas Cronin, *Direct Democracy* (Cambridge, Massachusetts, 1989)

General Collections

This map shows the extent to which American state governments by the mid-1980s had adopted the Swiss devices of initiative and referendum. Note the popularity of these instruments of direct democracy in the western part of the country.

> have written their laws in language so plain that a layman may be judge in the highest court. They have forestalled monopolies, improved and reduced taxation, avoided incurring heavy public debts, and have made a better distribution of their land than any other European country. They have practically given home rule in local affairs to every community. They have calmed disturbing political elements,—the press is purified, the politician disarmed, the civil service well regulated.[19]

For Allen and millions of other Americans the trail blazed in Switzerland was the way out of the hell of American life.

In the 1890s interest in the initiative and referendum was the keenest where conditions of American life were the harshest: in the factories and on the farms. The American Federation of Labor at its 1892 convention endorsed direct democracy in the following terms: "it finds the principle of direct legislation through the Initiative and Referendum approved by the experience of Switzerland as a most valuable auxiliary in securing an extension of the opportunities of the wage earning class."[20] The same year the Populist Party, whose core support was in the agrarian West, passed a similar endorsement at its national convention and became the principal vehicle for the adoption of Swiss direct democracy devices in American state governments.

Most initiative and referendum states, as a glance at a map will show, are in the western United States, in areas where the Populists were strongest. In 1898 South Dakota became the first state to adopt the initiative and referendum. Utah followed in 1900, Oregon in 1902. Of the eighteen states that adopted one or the other of these devices by 1912, sixteen were west of the Mississippi. Oregon reformers corresponded directly with Swiss experts like Professor Charles Borgeaud of the University of Geneva and Karl Burkli of Zurich who assured them that "Our Swiss political trinity—initiative, referendum, and proportional representation—is not only good and holy for hard-working Switzerland, but it would be even better . . . for the great country in North America."[21] That these testimonials had an impact is affirmed by a leading reformer who asserted: "I believe I do not overstate the fact when I say Oregon is wholly indebted to Switzerland for these tools of democracy."[22]

Successful though the movement for the initiative and referendum was in the states, it fared poorly on the national level. From the beginning many of its supporters thought that the size and complexity of the United States precluded direct democracy in the federal government. Reformers like Robert LaFollette and George Norris were willing to give the case for a national initiative and referendum a hearing, however, and in 1909 LaFollette introduced in the Senate a State Department report on the "Initiative in Switzerland."[23] The preceding year officials of the Initiative and Referendum League of America presented to Congress a memorial advocating federal adoption of these devices and supporting their case by citing the beneficent impact of direct democracy in the canton of Zurich from 1869 to 1893.[24] Congress listened, but took no action.

Between 1913 and 1918 five more states adopted either the initiative or the referendum. The First World War and the return to "normalcy" in the 1920s suffocated the reforming spirit in the United States and, according to a scholar writing in 1970, "took the wind out of the sails of the direct legislation movement [which] has not had a revival since."[25] This obituary was premature, however, for interest in direct democracy appears to have revived, stimulated, apparently, by the success of California's Proposition 13, an initiative in June 1978 which the residents of the Golden State used to cut their property taxes. Proposition 13 was imitated in other states and prompted politicians in states without the initiative to propose its establishment. In recent years movements for direct democracy have been mounted, with varying levels of popular support, in Alabama, Georgia, Hawaii, Minnesota, New Jersey, New York, Rhode Island, and Texas. In 1988 at least fifty initiatives were on the ballot in eighteen states.[26]

Contemporary proponents of the initiative and referendum cite successes in sister American states in making their cases. Most have forgotten that the sister republic, Switzerland, first inspired the adoption of these devices in the United States.

NOTES

1. William E. Rappard, "The Initiative, Referendum and Recall in Switzerland," American Academy of Political and Social Sciences, *Annals*, 43 (September 1912), 125–6.
2. *Ibid.*, 126.
3. W. D. McCrackan, "The Swiss Referendum, The Ideal Republican Government," *The Cosmopolitan*, 15 (July 1893), 333.
4. Hans R. Guggisberg, "The Unusual American Career of the Swiss Politician Emil Frey (1838–1922)," Swiss American Historical Society, *Newsletter*, 22 (June 1986), 18–19.
5. Ellis P. Oberholtzer, *The Referendum in America* (New York, 1900), v.
6. Rappard, "Initiative, Referendum and Recall," op. cit., 118–121.
7. *Ibid.*, 123.
8. Sullivan, *Direct Legislation*, iii.
9. *Ibid.*, iv.

10. Heinz K. Meier, *Friendship under Stress: U.S.–Swiss Relations 1900–1950* (Bern, 1970), 18.
11. *Referendum News*, 1 (Aug. 1906), 37.
12. Albert Bartholdi, compiler, *Prominent Americans of Swiss Origin* (New York, 1932), 84.
13. James W. Sullivan, "Direct Legislation in Switzerland," *Direct Legislation Record*, 1 (September 1894), 67.
14. Sullivan, *Direct Legislation, op. cit.*, 15.
15. *Ibid.*, 95.
16. Sullivan, "Direct Legislation in Switzerland," *op. cit.*, 67.
17. Henry E. Allen, *In Hell and the Way Out*, (Chicago, 1896), 9–10.
18. *Ibid.*, 13.
19. *Ibid.*, 21.
20. George H. Shibley, *A Brief Review of Organized Labor's Non-Partisan Campaign for Majority Rule* (Washington, 1902), 5.
21. Senate Document, 529, May 29, 1908. *Supplemental Memorial of Initiative and Referendum League of America relating to National Initiative and Referendum*, 18.
22. Rappard, "Initiative, Referendum, and Recall," *op. cit.*, 125.
23. Senate Document 126, July 13, 1909.
24. Senate Document, 516, May 25, 1908.
25. Meier, *Friendship under Stress*, op. cit., 20.
26. Thomas Cronin, *Direct Democracy: The Politics of Initiative, Referendum, and Recall* (Cambridge, Massachusetts, 1989), 3.

Afterword

The term, sister republic, is not used today to describe relations between the United States and Switzerland. As late as the 1960s one could hear Swiss and Americans describing each others' countries as sister democracies,[1] but the venerable phrase, sister republic, appears to have become obsolete. To a contemporary ear it may even sound contrived, having the ring of a catchy but empty phrase invented to drum up interest in an anniversary celebration.

The phrase, however, was anything but empty in the nineteenth century when the United States and Switzerland saw themselves as kindred polities, republics alone in a menacing world of monarchs and autocrats. Though it would be an exaggeration to say that in the nineteenth century Switzerland and the United States had a "special relationship" of the kind enjoyed by the United States and Britain in the immediate post World War II period, the two countries were conscious that they shared historical experiences—both having survived similar civil wars—and that they shared institutional features, established by reciprocal borrowing.

The sense of shared political distinctiveness, which created bonds between the United States and Switzerland, disappeared with the proliferation of republics after the First and Second World Wars. Today, the world is full of "republics," some models of good government, others more tyrannical than the most despotic eighteenth century monarchy. This explosion of republics has created a political universe in which Switzerland and the United States are no longer exceptional and no longer feel the closeness that such singularity creates.

The Second World War further undercut the sense of community between the United States and Switzerland. Many Americans, taking a simplistic view of foreign politics, thought that the Swiss, by practicing their traditional policy of neutrality, had tilted too far toward Germany. In abandoning its own long-standing policy of neutrality by joining the North Atlantic Treaty Organization in 1949, the United States acquired a new set of European friends, who became the focus of its attention. Switzerland no longer held a special place in the American field of vision and the concept of the sister republic suffered accordingly.

The term, nevertheless, reminds us of the significant contributions the United States and Switzerland have made to each others' institutions. In recognition of these mutual contributions and with profound admiration for 700 years of Swiss independence and freedom the Library of Congress, reviving a happy phrase, salutes the Sister Republic.

NOTES

1. For the term sister democracy, see Alfred Zehnder (Swiss Ambassador to the U.S.), speech, April 28, 1964, at Suffolk University, Boston, printed in *Amerikanische Schweizer Zeitung*, July 1–8, 1964, and a statement of the American Society for Friendship with Switzerland, Inc., 1966, quoted in Meier, *Friendship under Stress, op. cit.*, 391.

François D'Ivernois (1757–1842)

Silhouette, ca. 1800

Artist unknown

Fearful that the University of Geneva and its faculty would be destroyed by political revolutionaries in the summer of 1794, D'Ivernois devised a plan to transplant L'Académie de Calvin to the United States. He proposed that the University be established near the new city of Washington and be made the national university of the new republic.

Addendum

The Founding Fathers and the University of Geneva: The Project to Purchase "L'Académie de Calvin"

Geneva occupied a special place in the hearts of eighteenth-century Americans. Many traced their spiritual roots to the city that had served as an engine of the Protestant Reformation and had given John Calvin his pulpit. Revolutionary leaders such as Henry Laurens and Benjamin Franklin sent their children and grandchildren to Geneva to be educated in a properly Protestant intellectual and religious environment. So high was the Revolutionary generation's esteem for Geneva that the first four presidents of the United States—the cream of the Founding Fathers—explored ways to buy, first with public funds and then with George Washington's private fortune, the University of Geneva—"L'Académie de Calvin"—and move it to the United States.

"The splendid project," as Thomas Jefferson called it, of "transplanting the academy of Geneva" to the United States—"toute entière, toute organizée, et avec elle tous les moyens d'instruction"[1]—was the brainchild of François D'Ivernois (1757–1842), a Genevois of French Huguenot descent, whose life was a carousel of changing fortunes, politics, vocations, and loyalties.[2] D'Ivernois attended the University of Geneva from 1773 to 1777, where he was a classmate of Albert Gallatin, the most famous and influential of all Swiss immigrants to the United States. The precocious D'Ivernois established a publishing house upon graduating from college and in 1779 printed the first comprehensive edition of the writings of Jean-Jacques Rousseau, a friend of his father. In 1781 D'Ivernois

---

This addendum, new to the second edition, constitutes the only substantial change from the original 1991 edition.

enthusiastically participated in the overthrow of Geneva's aristocratic party and, when France, Sardinia, and Bern forcibly restored the aristocrats the next year, the young revolutionary was exiled from his native city.

Armed with letters of introduction from a well-placed British diplomat, D'Ivernois travelled to Great Britain in 1782, where he lived for most of the next thirty years. He spent his first years in Britain trying to persuade the king's ministers to provide land and financial subsidies to settle politically disaffected Genevois watchmakers and jewellers in Ireland.

When it became obvious, by 1785, that a New Geneva would not be established in Ireland, D'Ivernois considered emigrating to America. Encouraged by Richard Price and other British liberals, who regarded him as a martyr to liberty, D'Ivernois discussed his plans in Paris in 1785 with Thomas Jefferson, American ambassador to the court of Louis XVI. By the late 1780s D'Ivernois began to drift away from his earlier political liberalism. He accepted a pension from the British government and befriended John Adams, American minister to the court of St. James. D'Ivernois was attracted to Adams's political philosophy, as articulated in the *Defence of the Constitutions . . . of the United States of America (1787)*.[3] In that work Adams assailed the democracy D'Ivernois had previously favored and offered as an alternative the ancient theory of mixed and balanced government.

A turn of the political wheel permitted D'Ivernois to go back to Geneva in February 1790. He held public office and participated in negotiations with the commander of a French army threatening the city. He became, however, increasingly disillusioned with the radicalization of Geneva politics and returned to London at the end of 1793, denouncing the Genevois for repudiating their balanced constitution.

Geneva plunged into Hell, D'Ivernois believed, on 18 July 1794, when radicals seized the government and established a revolutionary tribunal on the French model. In a purge lasting 18 days, the tribunal handed down 508 sentences, ranging from death (37) to exile to house arrest. Viewing "the Arts and Sciences as branches of Aristocracy," the revolutionaries made the Academy of Geneva a particular target, "imprisoning many of the Professors and almost the whole of the Clergy."[4] Receiving this news in London, D'Ivernois feared that his alma mater would be consumed, at any moment, by a revolutionary holocaust and set to work with manic energy to save the university from annihilation. The United States, D'Ivernois desperately hoped, would rescue the University of Geneva by adopting a plan inspired by his earlier efforts to settle

Geneva's watchmakers in Ireland. Now D'Ivernois proposed to remove, not craftsmen, but an entire university to a foreign land.

On 22 August 1794, D'Ivernois published an impassioned pamphlet, *La Révolution française à Genève,* which described the atrocities of the revolutionaries and their French masters, "the cruel authors of all our misery." D'Ivernois dedicated the pamphlet to "an American" (John Adams) and circulated it in the United States to arouse sympathy for his "unhappy Countrymen [who] are about to embark for America in confidence of finding there, the liberty and security which they have lost at home." The Genevois "who settle among you," D'Ivernois informed his American readers, will "bring your habits of acting and thinking, truly Republican, and perfectly conformable to your own."[5] The same day D'Ivernois dispatched to his friend John Adams, now vice president of the United States, and to his old classmate, Albert Gallatin, who had recently represented Pennsylvania in the United States Senate, his proposal for transplanting the university. On 5 September 1794, the day on which he was sentenced to death in absentia by the revolutionary tribunal in Geneva, D'Ivernois sent his plan to Thomas Jefferson, now a private citizen after three years service as the first American secretary of state.

What D'Ivernois proposed was this: the American federal government or one of the individual states would sell uncultivated lands worth approximately $300,000 to a company of Geneva investors that he, D'Ivernois, would organize. From the proceeds of this sale, $50,000 would be used to build a university campus; the remainder would become an endowment fund, invested in United States government securities, to yield $15,000 per year to support the professors and their families. Anticipating objections that his plan was a "belle chimère," D'Ivernois assured his American correspondents that he could recruit the necessary investors and that the faculty of the university would be eager to escape the perils of Geneva. Although his negotiations with the professors were conducted in secrecy (to prevent reprisals against them), there is no doubt that they were receptive to his propositions.

The first response from America was disappointing, doubly so since it came from Gallatin. The plan would not work, Gallatin informed D'Ivernois on 23 December 1794. He had, accordingly, taken the liberty to devise a better solution, creating a New Geneva Company which would buy land in the wilderness of northeastern Pennsylvania and sell it, not to university professors, but to emigrating artisans and craftsmen. D'Ivernois objected to Gallatin's initiative as a land speculating scheme, subversive of his own humanitarian objectives. The politics of Geneva may have crossed the Atlantic

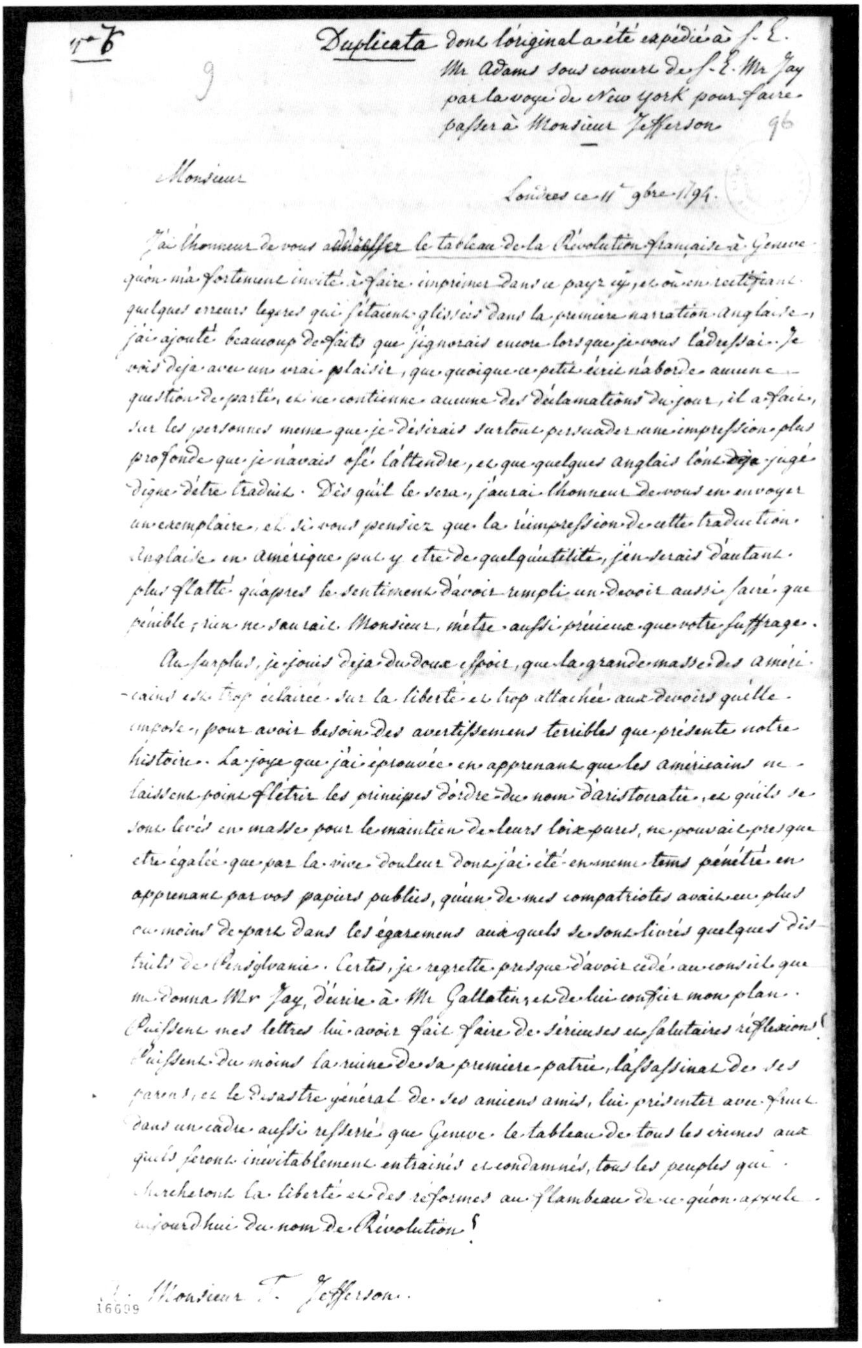

N° 6

Duplicata dont l'original a été expédié à S. E. Mr Adams sous couvert de S. E. Mr Jay par la voye de New York pour faire passer à Monsieur Jefferson

9

96

Monsieur

Londres ce 11 9bre 1794.

J'ai l'honneur de vous addresser le tableau de la Révolution françaide à Geneve qu'on m'a fortement invité à faire imprimer dans ce pays ci, et où en rectifiant quelques erreurs legeres qui s'étaient glissées dans la premiere narration Anglaise, j'ai ajouté beaucoup de faits que j'ignorais encore lorsque je vous l'adressai. Je vois deja avec un vrai plaisir, que quoique ce petit écrit n'aborde aucune question de parti, et ne contienne aucune des déclamations du jour, il a fait, sur les personnes meme que je désirais surtout persuader une impression plus profonde que je n'avais osé l'attendre, et que quelques Anglais l'ont deja jugé digne d'etre traduit. Dès qu'il le sera, j'aurai l'honneur de vous en envoyer un exemplaire, et si vous pensiez que la réimpression de cette traduction Anglaise en Amérique put y etre de quelqu'utilité, j'en serais d'autant plus flatté qu'après le sentiment d'avoir rempli un devoir aussi sacré que pénible, rien ne saurait, Monsieur, m'etre aussi précieux que votre suffrage.

Au surplus, je jouis deja du doux espoir, que la grande masse des Américains est trop éclairée sur la liberté et trop attachée aux devoirs qu'elle impose, pour avoir besoin des avertissemens terribles que présente notre histoire. La joye que j'ai éprouvée en apprenant que les Américains ne laissent point flétrir les principes d'ordre du nom d'aristocratie, et qu'ils se sont levés en masse pour le maintien de leurs loix pures, ne pouvait presque etre égalée que par la vive douleur dont j'ai été en meme tems pénétré en apprenant par vos papiers publics, qu'un de mes compatriotes avait eu plus ou moins de part dans les égaremens auxquels se sont livrés quelques districts de Pensylvanie. Certes, je regrette presque d'avoir cédé au conseil que me donna Mr Jay, d'écrire à Mr Gallatin, et de lui confier mon plan. Puissent mes lettres lui avoir fait faire de sérieuses et salutaires réflexions! Puissent du moins la ruine de sa premiere patrie, l'assassinat de ses parens, et le désastre général de ses anciens amis, lui présenter avec fruit dans un cadre aussi resserré que Geneve le tableau de tous les crimes auxquels seront inévitablement entrainés et condamnés, tous les peuples qui chercheront la liberté et des réformes au flambeau de ce qu'on appele aujourd'hui du nom de Révolution!

A Monsieur T. Jefferson.

16699

François D'Ivernois to Thomas Jefferson, 11 November 1794

Holograph

Thomas Jefferson Papers, Manuscript Division

This letter furnishes evidence of the influential Americans who supported D'Ivernois's project. Written to Jefferson, an ardent proponent of transplanting the University of Geneva, it was sent to America, as the note in the upper right corner indicates, under diplomatic cover by Chief Justice John Jay to Vice President John Adams, both advocates of D'Ivernois's plan. In the letter D'Ivernois denounces Albert Gallatin, whose support he had tried to enlist, for embracing in America the kind of ultra-democratic politics that were ruining Geneva.

and poisoned relations between Gallatin and D'Ivernois, for Gallatin's close associate, a fellow Genevois named Jean Badollet, took the egalitarian line of the Geneva radicals, ridiculing D'Ivernois's plan as a measure to promote the "welfare of the wealthy" and blasting the university's professors "as mere linguists and rhetors and a set of babblers in politics."[6] D'Ivernois, in the meantime, had learned of Gallatin's involvement in riots in western Pennsylvania, called the Whiskey Rebellion, and told Jefferson he regretted dealing with someone who seemed to be imitating the incendiaries in Geneva.

Unlike D'Ivernois's countrymen, Americans responded to his proposals for an "Emigration of the Academy of Geneva" with unrestrained enthusiasm. As John Adams informed D'Ivernois in April 1795: "all acknowledge the honour it would do us, and the advantages which would result to us."[7] A golden opportunity, it seemed, had been unexpectedly laid on the new republic's doorstep. Chief Justice John Jay, who was in London in 1794 on a special mission to conclude a commercial treaty with Great Britain, was charmed by D'Ivernois—perhaps because of a common Huguenot background—and acted as his advisor, urging him to go to the United States and to negotiate personally the transfer of the university. Adams did all that he could to help D'Ivernois, circulating his proposal to leading politicians, including President Washington, who pronounced the situation in Geneva "afflicting" and D'Ivernois's ideas "important,"[8] and Secretary of State Edmund Randolph, who excitedly declared that "to the utmost of my faculties I would welcome them [the Genevois] to our country with the most zealous hospitality" because the "transportation of [the] academy would fill up a vast chasm in the education of the United States."[9]

Randolph's enthusiasm was exceeded by that of Thomas Jefferson, normally the most reserved of men. D'Ivernois bombarded Jefferson with letters (thirteen between September 1794 and March 1795),[10] imploring him to become the "Protector" of the University of Geneva. These pleas struck a chord in Jefferson, who was temporarily retired from politics, and aroused him to try to accomplish D'Ivernois's objectives. To the third president, the importance of acquiring the University of Geneva was indisputable. "The colleges of Geneva and Edinburgh," he wrote Washington, are "the two eyes of Europe in matters of science;" Geneva, Jefferson added, surpassed its Scotch rival in everything but medicine.[11] If the University of Geneva could be transferred to northern Virginia, as D'Ivernois proposed, Jefferson "would have seen with peculiar satisfaction the establishment of such a mass of science in my country, and should probably have been tempted to approach myself to it, by procuring a residence in its neighborhood at those

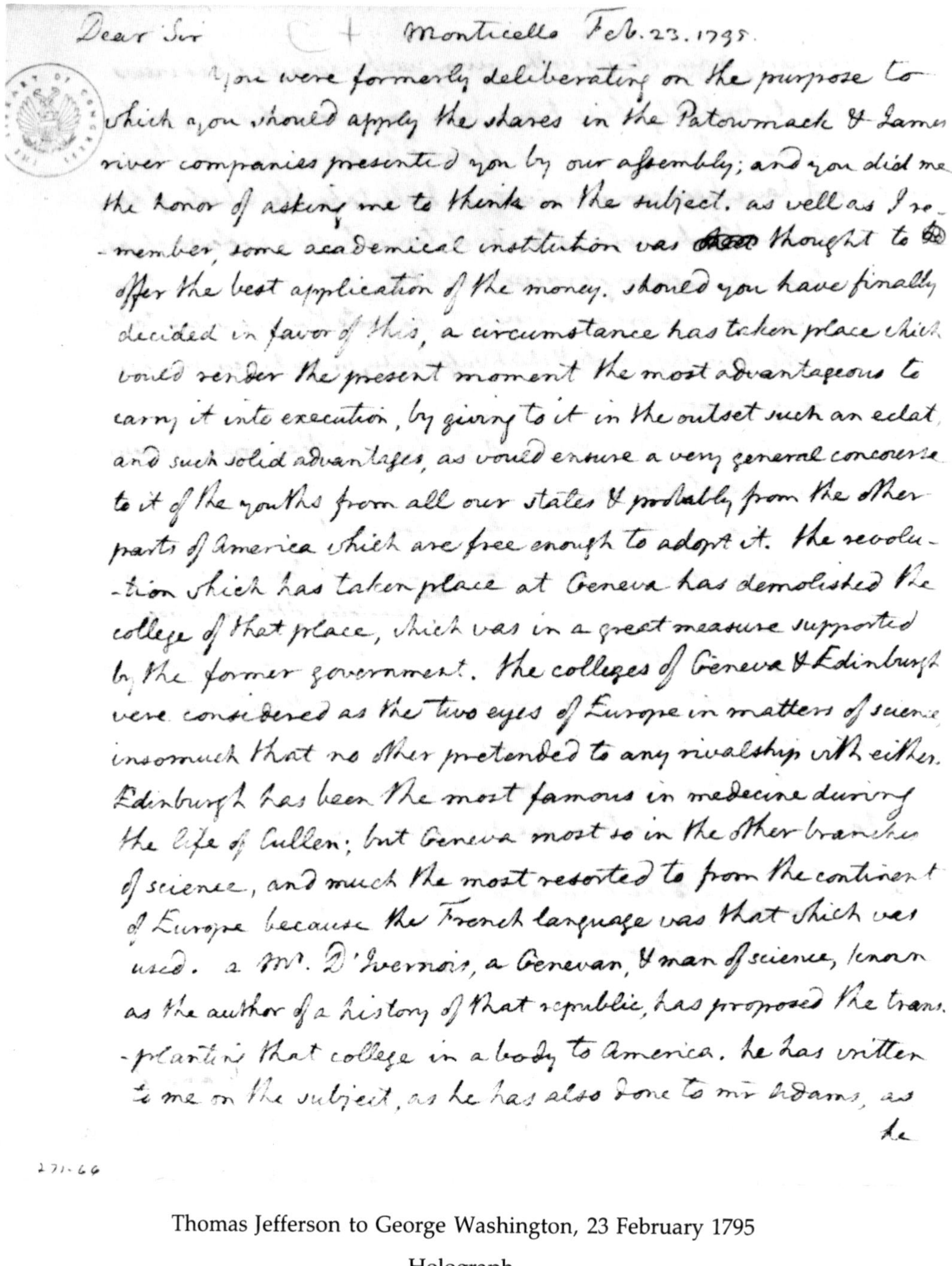

Dear Sir C + Monticello Feb. 23. 1795.

You were formerly deliberating on the purpose to which you should apply the shares in the Patowmack & James river companies presented you by our assembly; and you did me the honor of asking me to think on the subject. as well as I re-member, some academical institution was thought to offer the best application of the money. should you have finally decided in favor of this, a circumstance has taken place which would render the present moment the most advantageous to carry it into execution, by giving to it in the outset such an eclat, and such solid advantages, as would ensure a very general concourse to it of the youths from all our states & probably from the other parts of America which are free enough to adopt it. the revolu-tion which has taken place at Geneva has demolished the college of that place, which was in a great measure supported by the former government. the colleges of Geneva & Edinburgh were considered as the two eyes of Europe in matters of science insomuch that no other pretended to any rivalship with either. Edinburgh has been the most famous in medecine during the life of Cullen; but Geneva most so in the other branches of science, and much the most resorted to from the continent of Europe because the French language was that which was used. a Mr. D'Ivernois, a Genevan, & man of science, known as the author of a history of that republic, has proposed the trans-planting that college in a body to America. he has written to me on the subject, as he has also done to mr Adams, as he

Thomas Jefferson to George Washington, 23 February 1795

Holograph

George Washington Papers, Manuscript Division

Praising the University of Geneva as one of the "two eyes of Europe in matters of science," Jefferson urges President George Washington to use his private fortune to provide funds to bring the University to the United States.

seasons of the year when the operations of agriculture are less active and interesting."[12] Jefferson, in other words, would have routinely left his precious Monticello to become a kind of patron in residence at the new university; had he done so, he surely would have seen no reason to found, as he did some years later, the University of Virginia, one of his proudest accomplishments.

Jefferson instructed a political lieutenant, Wilson Cary Nicholas, to sound out in confidence leading members of the Virginia General Assembly to gauge their interest in buying the University of Geneva. In February 1795 Nicholas informed Jefferson that he had made the desired overtures and had discovered that, although the members "were generally well disposed to the proposition, and some of them warmly,"[13] the Assembly was unwilling to vote the necessary funds. Jefferson was offended by this response and mocked the Virginia Assembly for its short-sightedness. He next wrote Washington (23 February 1795)[14] and asked the president to put up some of his own money—he could sell stock in a canal company, Jefferson suggested—to underwrite the costs of bringing the University of Geneva to the United States. Washington conferred with his closest advisors, including the "Father of the Constitution," James Madison, who became the fourth president in 1809. Madison was impressed with the advantages of Jefferson's proposal, but the unfortunate fact was that Washington had pledged his canal shares to another educational venture. With this rebuff, Jefferson ceased his efforts to acquire L'Académie de Calvin.

D'Ivernois made one last demarche on behalf of his project, proposing to Jefferson, 21 March 1795, that if the University of Geneva were established in northern Virginia, near the new capital city arising on the banks of the Potomac, it would be appropriate to make "notre Université, l'Université Fedérative de l'Amerique."[15] Lest D'Ivernois be accused of succumbing to megalomania, it should be noted that Secretary of State Randolph suggested to John Adams, 11 November 1794, that the University of Geneva be settled in the new federal city.

On this audacious note D'Ivernois's efforts to save his beloved university ended. By the beginning of 1795 politics in Geneva had become more civil and the professors no longer feared for their lives. In 1796 D'Ivernois was publicly exposed by enemies in Britain as a royal pensioner, information which undermined his credibility with Jefferson and his partisans, who had taken an anti-British posture in domestic politics. With his friend John Adams, by 1796 a political opponent of Jefferson, D'Ivernois continued to exchange letters, even after Adams was elected second president in 1797. The University of Geneva ceased, however, to be a topic of their correspondence.

The project to purchase the University of Geneva reveals the high mutual respect in which Americans and Genevois held each other at the end of the eighteenth century. The first four presidents of the United States and other distinguished Founding Fathers like Jay and Randolph supported—some with great ardor—the plan to bring L'Académie de Calvin across the Atlantic. D'Ivernois and his conservative circle paid the United States the ultimate compliment of proposing to emigrate to it; their admiration for the new nation was matched, however, by that of their revolutionary adversaries who, to D'Ivernois's disgust, displayed the American flag alongside their own at a great Civic Feast in Geneva on 1 September 1794. The broad reciprocal respect between the United States and Geneva—and between the United States and other parts of Switzerland—was the fertile soil from which, during the nineteenth century, the concept of the Sister Republics blossomed and flourished.

NOTES

1. Thomas Jefferson to John Adams, 6 February 1795, Adams Papers, Massachusetts Historical Society; François D'Ivernois to Thomas Jefferson, 5 September 1794, Jefferson Papers, Library of Congress. The Adams and Jefferson Papers have been microfilmed and may be borrowed from the Library of Congress through the inter-library loan system.
2. All facts about D'Ivernois's life that appear in this chapter, unless otherwise indicated, are derived from Otto Karmin, *Sir Francis D'Ivernois 1757–1842 Sa Vie, Son Oeuvre et Son Temps* (Geneva, 1920). Karmin's work is a Ph.D. dissertation which takes a debunking attitude toward its subject. Karmin is unsympathetic to D'Ivernois on ideological grounds and depreciates his achievements, especially his efforts to remove the University of Geneva to America. Karmin, moreover, has a limited knowledge of American sources and of American political conditions. The result is an incomplete and unsatisfactory account of a complex and important episode in American-Swiss relations.
3. See, for example, D'Ivernois to Adams, 30 January 1787, 18 June 1790, Adams Papers, Massachusetts Historical Society.
4. François D'Ivernois, *A Short Account of the Late Revolution in Geneva . . . in a Series of Letters to an American* (London, 1795), 25, 58.
5. *Ibid.*, 39.
6. Jean Badollet to Albert Gallatin, 18 June 1795, Albert Gallatin Papers, microfilm edition, reel 3, Library of Congress.
7. Adams to D'Ivernois, 26 April 1795, Adams Papers, Massachusetts Historical Society.
8. George Washington to John Adams, 15 November 1794, Adams Papers, Massachusetts Historical Society.
9. Edmund Randolph to John Adams, 16 November 1794, ibid.
10. These may be found in the Jefferson Papers, Library of Congress.

11. Thomas Jefferson to George Washington, 23 February 1795, Washington Papers, Library of Congress.
12. Jefferson to D'Ivernois, 6 February 1795, Jefferson Papers, Library of Congress; this letter has been reprinted in Paul L. Ford, ed., *The Works of Thomas Jefferson*, 8 (New York, 1904), 163-6.
13. Ibid.
14. See note 11, supra.
15. This D'Ivernois letter to Jefferson of 21 March 1795 exists in a copy in the Adams Papers.

⊗ "The paper used in this publication meets the minimum requirements of American National Standard for Information Sciences—Permanence of Paper for Printed Library Materials, ANSI Z39.48-1984."

Designed by William Chenoweth